Dangling

晃 荡

Dangling

晃 荡

Yang Xie

杨邪

Translated by Ouyang Yu

译者 ： 欧阳昱

PUNCHER & WATTMANN

© Yang Xie 2019

Cover image: Zhao Baokang

First published in 2019

Published by Puncher and Wattmann

PO Box 279

Warath NSW 2298

Australia

http://www.puncherandwattmann.com

puncherandwattmann@bigpond.com

ISBN 9781925780208

NATIONAL
LIBRARY
OF AUSTRALIA

A catalogue record for this book is available
from the National Library of Australia

Contents

某个下午

某个下午
有位我一直热恋着的诗人
他的第五本诗集
居然让我一下子从中闻出了
一股
类似耗子的气味

某个下午
一本刚买的大诗刊
被我撕得稀烂
一份刚到的众所周知的报纸
被我携往厕所

某个下午
嚼了八颗劣质糖果
写成一首口语诗
比数年前练习册上的诗们
还诗

某个下午

传闻中的一粒铅弹

从一管汽枪中激动地

射出

快活击中眼前那女人

丰腴摆动的臀部

某个下午

看见自己走上街道

挤操了一阵

最终记不起去干什么

悻悻地回来

某个下午

电视里毫无节目

耐心细听

一个枯燥的讲话结束

像听一篇关于空难的报道

津津有味

某个下午

去睡觉

睡不着
盯住床顶
后来梦中紧咬牙关
两耳轰鸣
天旋地转
晕倒在哪个荒冈
一边警告自己
这就是写作的后果
又该去买药了

某个下午
很平常

On a Certain Afternoon

on a certain afternoon
I, on a sudden, actually smelt something
like a rat
from the fifth collection of poetry
by a poet
I had been passionately in love with

on a certain afternoon
a mass poetry magazine, just bought
was ripped to pieces by me
and a newspaper, known to all, that had just arrived
was carried by me to the toilet

on a certain afternoon
I chewed eight bad-quality candies
and wrote an oral poem
that was more poetry
than the poems written on an exercise book several years ago

on a certain afternoon
a lead bullet, as rumour would have it
was shot
excitedly from an air gun

that hit the swaying plumpness

of the hips of a woman in front of me

on a certain afternoon

I saw myself walking on a street

and being crowded about for a while

still, I did not know what I was going to do

so I came home in dejection

on a certain afternoon

there were no programs on TV

and when you listened carefully

to a dry speech end itself

you quite enjoyed yourself

as if you were listening to a report about an air crash

on a certain afternoon

you went to sleep

but found you couldn't

staring, as you were, at the top of the bed

and, later, in a dream, you clenched your teeth

your ears ringing

feeling as if the heavens were turning

as you fell on a deserted ridge

reminding yourself that

this was the consequence of writing

and that you had to go and buy some medications again

on a certain afternoon

a very ordinary one

唤声

有个声音说
"喂，你来，你来……"
在我前面

她是谁
是谁在唤我
我摸黑循声紧随着走

终而到一个亮处
终而让我给跟上了

而却竟是个疯子
她转过身
仍吃吃地笑
"喂，你来，你来……"

Calling

ahead of me
a voice is saying
'hello, you, come over, come over...'

who is she
who is it that is calling me
groping in the dark, I follow it closely

till I arrive at a light spot
and find it

but it's a mad woman
she turns around
still giggling
'hello, you, come, come over...'

诗

是谁，是什么时候
让我踏上这条路
冥冥中径直对着这个方向？
还是这仅仅是，一次
偶然的拦截？

其实任何的探问，或者玄想
俱都毫无意义
这冥冥中的房子
现在我早已走入，禁锢多年
我早已是一个，完全的囚徒

我挣扎在感觉与感觉之间
这叫漫步
在这房子局促的空间
我抛掷一些，语词的意象
这叫飞翔
当我一阵阵痉挛，虚脱
跌坐于地
我是王

自己放风的一个个一瞬
是吃力打开一扇一扇，小小的囚窗
我看见原野，看见村庄
我看见河边快活挥汗的人们
我看见一片片白色的建筑，看见
一片片，亢奋的喧嚣

却始终看不清我那条路径，或许
它早已消逝

Poetry

who got me to step onto this road
and when, directly in this direction
in the unseen world?
was this the only one
accidental interception?

in fact, any enquiry, or meditation
is meaningless
in the house of this unseen world
that I entered, I have been imprisoned
I have long been a complete prisoner

I struggle between feeling and feeling
which is called strolling
in the cramped space of this house
I throw, worded images
which is called flying
in my spasms, and collapses
and when I fall sitting down on the ground
I am a king

the moments in which I let myself out for fresh air
are small windows I struggle, to open

I see the plain, see the village

I see people sweating happily by the river

I see spreads of white buildings, see

spreads, delirious commotion

I can never clearly see my path, or perhaps it

has long disappeared

我看见

今天我看见
一个富人
我不知道他的脑和肠
究竟怎样
我只知道
他大腹便便面容油亮
对了有一点很重要
我突然分辨出了
他哪一只是左手
他哪一只是右手

今天我看见
一个女人
她浓妆的面具之后
是一张凄白的纸
仿佛轻轻的触摸
都会使它碎破
而她高高束起的乳房
竟然高一只低一只
而她近于透明的包裙之内

桃红的绣边裤衩
赫然匆忙穿反

今天我看见
一个老头
比我父亲更老
我看见他
一手拿着一个旧提袋
一手紧紧捂住了上腹
他的面色青白
满头大汗
还有嘴角
嘴角在不住地哆嗦

I Saw

today I saw
a rich man
I knew not what his brains and intestines
were like
all I knew was
he had a potbelly and his face, oily shiny
right, there was something important
I, on a sudden, was able to tell
which hand was his left
and which, his right

today I saw
a woman
a ghastly paper
behind her heavily made-up mask
something that might break
at the merest touch
and her breasts, highly bundled up
one taller than the other
and her peach-red laced brief
put on the wrong way in a hurry
showed through underneath her near-transparent skirt

today I saw

an old man

older than my dad

I saw him

one hand holding an old bag

and the other, pressed on his upper abdomen

he looked pale

his head covered in sweat

and the corner of his mouth

it kept quivering

激情时代

你们，就在我的身边
开始出发
多么帅的男子
多么醒目的女人

引擎拉响
你们，一下子划破这条黄昏的热闹大街

一刻钟后有人过来，说
前面拐角
一个男子死死抱住了那株歪脖子梧桐
一个女的，脑袋撞扁了整个垃圾箱
而十丈之外躺着一辆摩托车——
多牛气多漂亮的赛车
浑身，雪白

In an Age of Passion

you, right by my side
begin setting out
the man so smart
the woman so eye-catching

the engine started
you, cut open this street, sun-setting and busy, in one go

fifteen minutes later, someone came over, and said:
in a corner somewhere ahead
a man, in a dead embrace, was hugging a Wutong tree with a twisted neck
and a woman, her head had smashed in the whole bin
a motor-cycle lying metres away—
what a stunningly beautiful racer
with a body, snow-white

非法分子

非法分子是来自郊外的两条狗
一条是黄狗
另外一条，也是黄狗

它们相约闯入市区
在这条市区边缘的繁华的大街
互相追逐，互相亲昵
而后互相用力把它们的爱
在众目睽睽之下，赤裸裸呈现

它们的爱是那样激烈
那样的持久，难分难解
而且是在白天，是在白天的大街
所以不久即蔚为壮观

这场刻骨铭心的爱的终止
是因为它惹出了一起小小的交通阻塞
并且，它们这样站在街心
不免也大大有碍市容
闻讯赶来的两名面无表情的巡警

在强硬的驱赶无效之后
动用了他们腰间的警棍
然后把一阵抽搐昏死过去但却
依旧难分难解的它们抛上车，一起拉走

这场闹剧后来留下了半截
臭气四溢的大粪，撂在了街心
还有那个胖嘟嘟巡警的一句咕哝——

The Illegal Elements

the illegal elements were two dogs from the suburbs
one was a yellow dog
and the other one, also a yellow dog

they had made an appointment to storm the city
they were now chasing each other and being intimate with each other
in this busy street on the edge of the city
and then they strenuously revealed their naked love
to the eyes of the public

their love was so fierce
so lasting, so hard to separate in their entanglement
and it was during the day, on a street in broad daylight
that it soon became a grand spectacle

the termination of this heart-engraving love
was a small traffic jam that it had caused
and standing the way they did right in the heart of the street
very much affected the appearance of the city
two expressionless patrolling policemen who heard the news and hurried in
used their batons from under their belts
after trying in vain to forcibly drive them away

and threw them, convulsing and fainting, into the police car

still inseparable in their entanglement, and dragged them away together

this farce left half a piece of

shit that stank to the high heavens, lying in the heart of the street

as well as a murmur from the fat patrolling policeman—

夜晚的女人

夜晚的女人来自外地
或者，更远的外省

夜晚的女人如同我们
百般呵护的小妹
风姿绰约
脸蛋上永远贴着，快乐的笑靥

夜晚的女人充斥着
这个小小的城市
她们让这个小小的城市
布满异样的香气
并且让它在这样的气息里
迅速成为，筐中白纸包裹的苹果
案头托盘上久置的梨子

夜晚的女人走上夜晚的大街
她们血红的口唇开启，不断吮吸
一支碧绿的冰棍

而同时，在她们最为隐秘的部位
悄然淌下了腥腥腻腻的，汁液

The Night Women

the night women come from *waidi*
or more distant provinces
the night women are like our little sisters
that we protect in a hundred ways
with graceful bearing and charms

the night women flood this
small city
they spread this small city
with their peculiar fragrance
and let it in this atmosphere
rapidly becoming apples wrapped in white paper in the bamboo baskets
and pears that sit permanently on the trays on the desktop

the night women walk the night streets
their blood lips open, sucking on
bright green ice-lollies

and, meanwhile, the most secret places in them

quietly ooze liquids, fishy and oily

拒绝

拒绝一枚钉子
进入木板
深陷其中

拒绝一只苹果
开始
由内而外的腐烂

拒绝一首诗歌
被人吟咏
产生流传的倾向

拒绝一名女子
频频显露
暧昧十足的笑靥

拒绝一个孕妇
让这世界
再添一份热闹

拒绝一位母亲
渐渐走上
离开的道路

拒绝一根时针
永远跟踪
消逝的好时光

我们应该
找到拒绝的方法

Saying No

saying no to a nail
entering into a wooden board
getting deep stuck there

saying no to an apple
beginning
to rot from inside out

saying no to a poem
sung and developing a tendency
to become popular

saying no to a woman
frequently revealing
her ambiguous smiles

saying no to a pregnant woman
adding more noise
to this world

saying no to a mother
gradually
taking the road of departure

saying no to a hand on the clock

always following

the good but gone old days

we must find

more ways of saying no

与一个女人交谈

与一个女人交谈
在夏日的，凉爽的黄昏

我对她自然有点儿熟悉，并且
不妨说，知之甚多：她带着一个
不大漂亮的，正读小学二年级的女儿
她有过一场，特别浪漫的爱情，和婚姻
只是两年前与她的花猫一样的男人
私下里，分了居
她应该是那种老大不小的女人了
可是青春，竟然没有，离开她几步
她明眸皓齿，额上梳着可爱的刘海儿
脸蛋上整天敷着快乐的，笑靥
她的漂亮人见人妒
还有，她每天至少换两次衣服
她的举止和谈吐，能见出先天就有的涵养
她的身高适中，体态姣好
（请允许我避免涉及她的臀部，因为我怕
不小心会用出，一个可能不雅的形容词）

她表情生动地与我交谈

许多优雅风趣的言辞，伴着

如兰的口气，争相进入我的耳朵

我想除了她的面部肌肉，有些略微松弛

她真的无可挑剔，哪怕是

如此接近地与她，面对着审视

然而我渐渐，变得心不在焉

不知怎么，我毫无理由地想起了家中

快要正式结婚的妻子：她有

三个姐妹，一个为富不仁的哥哥

小时候她营养不良，个头矮小

上中学时头上扎马尾巴，穿打满补钉的裤子

而她总是对她的同学们说自己

不喜欢甚至，讨厌穿裙子

——多年以前我们刚刚认识的时候

我觉得她是一个，快乐的女孩子

因此她的一生也应该，充满幸福和笑语

可是对于她隐隐饱经沧桑的额头，我却大为不解

在那个夏日的凉爽的，黄昏

我与那个女人的那场交谈

结束得有些意外，因为，她终于

察觉到了我，莫名其妙的心不在焉
或许还有我内心的，一点儿坐立不安

当我在凉爽的黄昏大街，浑身大汗地
骑车狂奔，忽然醒悟临别时
她眼眸里一闪而逝的神情，应该叫作什么
而我的谎言是，多么的禁不起推敲——

她笑着说，你有事还是——要上厕所？
我有点儿结巴，摸着一串东西，向她晃了再晃
我说对，啊……不是，是丢了一把，钥匙……

Talking With a Woman

talking with a woman
on a cool summery evening

naturally, I knew her a little, and
actually quite well: she had a
not very pretty daughter, studying at Grade 2, in a primary school
she had a particularly romantic love, and marriage
except that two years earlier she had, privately
separated from her man, a flowery cat
she's the sort of woman not too old nor young
although youth still managed to cling to her somehow
bright eyes, shining teeth, and lovely fringe bangs on her forehead
a happy smile pasted on her face all day
her beauty making everyone jealous who saw her
and, she changed her clothes twice a day
one could see she had well-bred manners from the way she behaved and
      talked
she was of medium height, her figure nice
(I'll avoid making references to her hips, please, because I'm afraid
I might carelessly use an inelegant adjective)

vividly and expressively, she talked with me
words, elegant and interesting, vied with each other

in trying to enter my ears, accompanied with a breath of orchid

she was impeccable, I think, except her facial muscles

were slightly flaccid, even on closer

examination, so close to her

gradually, though, I grew absent-minded

as I, somehow, thought of my wife

about to get officially married: she had

three sisters and a rich but heartless brother

in her childhood, she was short, suffering from malnutrition

at middle school, she had a ponytail and wore heavily patched trousers

and she always told her classmates that she herself

disliked, even hated, wearing a skirt

—many years ago when we first met I found her a happy girl

and, for this reason, she should lead a life full of happiness and smiles
      although

I can't understand how she had a forehead scarred with vicissitudes

on that cool, summery evening

my conversation with the woman

ended rather unexpectedly, because she ended up

sensing that I was bafflingly absentminded

or that I was a little restless within

as I rode my bike in a wild rush, drenched in sweat

on the cool, summery street, I suddenly realised what the fleeting look in her eye could be called

and how my lies were far, from convincing—

she smiled and said: You've got something else to do or you want to go to

the loo

I stammered, and brought out something, which I flashed to her

I said: Yes, well, but, no, I've lost, a key...

上楼梯的女人

上楼梯的女人
和我在梯口相遇
她对我嫣然一笑

上楼梯的女人
她知道我是一个不合时宜的青年诗人
（据说这件事情她是偶然听闻）
这或许正是她经常报我一笑的缘由吧

上楼梯的女人
除了有一次在楼下向我证实她的听闻
之后从未再和我说过一句言语

上楼梯的女人
她已经到了风韵犹存的年龄
所幸腰身尚显灵活并且笑靥怡人

上楼梯的女人
挟一身淡淡的香气
先我一步跨上了楼梯

她使平常的梯道突然变得

陡峭狭窄光线黯淡

而由于错觉

我发现她的后背居然

长了两个丰腴耸动的乳房

上楼梯的女人

她转过两个梯角

我接下的发现应该不是错觉——

我发现一直在我眼前款款摆挪的

光滑油亮的皮短裙

它的线缝弯曲并

显得有点儿不够对称

同时竟露出了差不多即将开裂的

端倪

The Woman Going Upstairs

the woman going upstairs
ran into me at the staircase
and she smiled, prettily

the woman going upstairs
knows I am a young poet out of keeping with the times
(it's said she has heard about this by pure chance)
which is probably why she often smiles for me

the woman going upstairs
has never said a word to me
apart from once when she confirmed the rumour with me downstairs

the woman going upstairs
is at an age where her charms are going
except that her waist still seems supple enough and her smile, winning

the woman going upstairs
generated a bodyful of fragrance
and she was one step upstairs ahead of me
on a sudden, she made the ordinary staircase
appear steep, narrow and dim
and, in an illusion

I thought I saw two big breasts heaving

on her back

the woman going upstairs

turned two corners as she went up

what I found next wasn't

an illusion, I don't think—

I found the leather skirt, sleek and shiny

that had been swaying from side to side

had a row of stitches that weren't quite straight and

appeared asymmetrical enough

and, at the same time, there was a beginning of something

about to crack open

在菜市场碰上一位绝色美人

在菜市场碰上一位绝色美人
——可以想象这个时候的
菜市场是如何的肮脏
小贩们挥汗如雨动作夸张叫声响亮
大家脚下的水磨石地面湿漉又滑腻
整个偌大空间充斥着
异常复杂的咸咸腥腥让人不由得要想起
一听变质的鱼肉罐头里面的空余部分
而我手里刚刚从案板上提起的那只塑料袋
它装着的两斤大肉又是多么俗不可耐

在菜市场碰上一位绝色美人
——我现在要说的是
我所见到的下半部分——
两只绝对高傲但又不至于让你担心的白皮凉靴
其上是一条绝对无可挑剔的时兴的背带裤
——我不是说它的面料洁白光滑薄如蝉翼
——我不是说它的线缝挺括笔直不差丝毫
我要说的是它的肥瘦得体与线条柔美
我要说的是它的节奏明快与韵律和谐

我要说的是它的弹性与芬芳它的超尘脱俗卓然不群
我要说的是——我真的无法形容而任何形容
都是辞不达意不得要领让人浑身起疙瘩的冒犯唐突……

在菜市场碰上一位绝色美人
——我接下要说的是那当儿我多么想
来一个庸俗无比的比喻——
这是一朵含露怒放在浊世的白玫瑰
她的芬芳和绝色过分长久地盛开在刻薄的时光中
而刻薄的时光对于她的芬芳和绝色
竟然又是如此懦弱如此无能为力……

在菜市场碰上一位绝色美人
——可以想象这个时候的我
又是如何的感慨复叹息——
这是谁家的婆娘她接受了怎样一个男人的差遣
因而要踏入这每日的肮脏场所?
啊美人——这是谁家的绝色婆娘她让我
在菜市场一边手提大肉一边如此忍不住
用我卑微的目光一再抚摩她的白皮凉靴
一再抚摩她的时兴的背带裤然后要在
过去多少个回味无穷的日夜之后

为此痛快淋漓地写下我的赞美之歌

为此痛快淋漓地写下一首粗鄙而崇高的诗篇?

Meeting a Raving Beauty in the Vegetable Market

meeting a raving beauty in the vegetable market

—you can imagine how dirty the market was

at this particular moment

the vendors, dripping with sweat, were crying their wares loudly, with

    exaggerated gestures

the waterstone ground underneath their feet wet and slippery

the big space filled

with such a complicated salty and fishy smell, I thought of

the empty part of a tin of fish or pork gone bad

and the plastic bag that I had just picked up from the chopping board

containing the kilo of big meat that was so vulgar

meeting a raving beauty in the vegetable market

—what I'd like to say now

is the second part of what I saw—

the pair of white strappy leather sandals that were arrogant but that didn't

    worry you

topped by fashionable, impeccable trousers with braces

—I'm not saying its fabric was white, smooth and as thin as the cicada's

    wing

—I'm not saying its lines were straight and accurate

all I wanted to say is their properness and soft beauty

their forthright rhyme and harmonious rhythm

their elasticity, fragrance and remarkable uniqueness

and all I wanted to say—I really can't describe it, as any description

defeats its own purpose, inducing goose-bumps, offensive...

meeting a raving beauty in the vegetable market

—what I wanted to say further is how I wanted to

use a very vulgar metaphor—

that she's a white dewy rose, opening in a dirty world

that her fragrance and beauty staying open for too long in the acerbic time

and that the acerbic time was so weak and helpless

before her fragrance and beauty...

meeting a raving beauty in the vegetable market

—one can imagine how I, at this particular time

lamented and sighed

whose wife was this who had to step into this dirty place

by running daily errands for her man?

oh, beautiful woman—whose wife was this

who let me, carrying my big meat, caress her white leather sandals

with my abject eyes, again and again

and caress her fashionable braces before

I, many days and nights after, going over it again and again wrote my song of praise, with such passion, before

I wrote a vulgar and sublime poem, with such passion?

疯子回家

疯子黄春花
去年离家八月八
如今春天里返回家

疯子黄春花
家里已有一个上学的娃
没料想疯疯癫癫离了家
蓬头垢面衣不蔽体
一朝回到家
已是肚子挺着个大冬瓜

敢问黄春花黄春花
疯子黄春花孕妇黄春花
谁谁谁谁才是肚子里娃的爸

The Mad Woman Coming Home

the mad woman Yellow Spring Flower
who left home last August 8
and who came home this spring

the mad woman Yellow Spring Flower
has got a kid at home who attends school
but she left home as crazy as a loon
unkempt, dressed in rags, dirty and filthy
once she came home, though
her belly was like a white gourd

can I venture a question: Spring Flower
mad woman, pregnant woman, Yellow Spring Flower
who who who who is the dad?

抱怨

这是公元 2000 年酷暑的一个中午
由于热量的缘故，我们洗完澡
躺到床上，隔着半公尺的距离开始了抱怨

妻子先是抱怨卫生巾的质量每况愈下
随后就直奔事物的本源——
她抱怨那该死的例假，她抱怨
"为什么该守信用的总是不守信用而
不必守信用的怎么却如此地遵守信用？"
她抱怨她们女人的例假，简直到了
深恶痛绝的地步——她说"我多么愿意
是情窦未开的小女孩，或者干脆
让我一步到位，跨过更年期
跨过更年期早早做个干干净净的女人！"

这是公元 2000 年酷暑的一个中午
我们躺在床上，妻子的抱怨声情并茂
而作为一个而立之年的男子
我的抱怨，私下里也正不可开交——

我抱怨那该死的情欲和更该死的性欲
我抱怨那混账的造物主
"既然给男人装配了如此旺盛的
与生俱来的欲望，却又为何
要设置那么一些该死的樊篱？"
我抱怨——食欲让人一日三餐风雨无阻
为什么情欲和性欲，不能
让人做到兵来将挡水来土掩？
"如果我从此做一个内外兼修的
阳痿者，那么我将过上
一种怎样与众不同的崭新生活？"

这是公元 2000 年酷暑的一个中午
由于抱怨，由于我们极其形而下又极其
形而上的抱怨，我们
再也无法进行那不上不下的午睡
于是我们干脆拍屁股起床，赶紧一起升火做饭

Our Complaints

this was a hot summer noon in 2000

because of the heat, we had a shower

and lay in bed, beginning to complain across a distance of half a metre

first, my wife complained about the quality of pads going from bad to
   worse

then she went straight to the source of the matter—

she complained about her damned period and she said

'why doesn't the faithful keep faith

while the unfaithful is so faithful with its word?'

she said that her period was absolutely

disgusting—she said, 'How I wish

to be a girl before puberty or let me simply

step into the year of change

and across it, to be a clean woman early'

this was a hot summer noon in 2000

we were lying in bed, my wife's complaints exuberant

and, as a man of 30, an age of independence

my complaints were no less busy—

I hated the damned desire and, worse, the damned sex

I hated the God-damned Creator

who gave us the desire we were born with but why did He

set up those damned barriers?'

I complained—that I could eat three meals a day without hindrance

but why when it comes to sexual desire

there is no stopping it?

'if I turned myself into an impotent person today

cultivated within and without, what kind of new life

would I live that is totally different from others?'

this was a hot summer noon in 2000

because of our complaints, our downward

and upward complaints, we were no longer

able to continue our nap, suspended in the air

so, we got up, patting ourselves on the bums, and prepared the lunch in a

    hurry

可疑

一个老头
七老八十的老头
没有患上老年痴呆
却站在那里
挥舞着手臂
情绪激昂
侃侃而谈

对不起了，老头
可疑的老头
我已经忍无可忍
欲冲上前去
完成一个
漂亮的下流动作——

我要一把褪下
您的——裤子
看个——究竟！

The Dubious Old Man

an old man
an old man in his seventies or eighties
not inflicted with dementia
but standing there
brandishing his arms
full of passion
speaking with fervor and assurance

I'm sorry, old man
dubious old man
I can't stand this any more
and I'm about to rush forward
to perform a beautiful dirty action—

I'll pull down your—pants
in one go
and see
what is really there!

恶心与幽默

这是一首比较恶心的诗
因为我没法不恶心
因为今儿个早上
墨黑的环城河里漂起了
一具雪白的女尸

观者如潮，脑血栓一样
堵塞了狭窄的老环城路
（这个小小的城市
饲养了太多闲人）
有人由于恶心而呕吐
但没有人由于呕吐而离开
因为这是一个几乎
浑身赤裸的少女……

而我留下是因为后来
警察有了幽默的发现——
他嘟着厚嘴唇说："真奇怪，她
怎么竟然，戴了两个乳罩？"

此刻的我真想骂娘——

"妈的，你是装蒜还是

脑袋里装了一盆糨糊？"

可这话到了嘴边

变成了一个吹向警察耳边的叹息

"不知是哪家夜总会

又失踪了，一名外地来的小姐……"

——但是警察他白了我一眼

仍然无动于衷

他仍然迷惑于另一个

平空多余出的乳罩，仍然在

喃喃自语："为什么，会多出这个？

这是个不容忽视的问题……"

此时此刻，我真的想学一学

港片里的那些警察哥儿的神情

我真的想上去拍拍他肩膀

然后竖起一个大拇指说：

"啊，师兄，你真幽默！

可是你知不知道，为什么

你每天要在腰上

佩上这不装子弹的玩意儿？"

Nausea and Humour

this is a quite disgusting poem
because I can't help feeling disgusted
because this morning
a snow-white female body
was floating in the inky river encircling the city

a tide of audience, like the cerebral thrombosis
had blocked the narrow, old road encircling the city
(this small city has fed
too many nothing-to-do people)
one vomited because of nausea
but no one left because of the vomit
because this was a nearly
naked girl…

I stayed because, later on
the policeman had made a humorous discovery—
he said, his thick lips pouting, 'It's so strange that she
should be wearing two bras.'

by then I would have blurted out with 'You mother fucker!
are you pretending or
is your brain full of paste?'

if the words had not turned into a sigh that blew into the ears of the
    policeman
when they arrived at my lips:
'don't know which nightclub this involves
but another *xiaojie* from outside this city has gone missing'
—but the policeman looked at me with disdain
remaining unmoved
still puzzled by the extra bra, still murmuring
to himself, 'Why, an extra one?
an issue not to be ignored…'

there and then, I really would have liked
to walk up to him and pat him on the shoulder
the way cops do in a Hong Kong film
and say, with my thumb up:
'oh, Brother, you are so funny!
but do you know why
you wear this thing on your belt every day
without the bullets?'

Translator's note—*xiaojie*, Little Sister, a prostitute

一个男人死了

一个男人死了
一个帅呆了的男人
有一天坐了一辆摩的
脑袋撞上了街边的一棵
新埋的漂亮的路灯杆

一个男人死了
他有一辆霸气十足的蓝色宝马
为什么心血来潮去坐摩的
这不重要
重要的是除了宝马
他还有两套四室一厅的房子
他还有一个娇艳惹火得令人立刻
联想到一张大床的妻子

我想起有一次去摁他家门铃
我摁一单元的 302 可他在二单元的 303
后来我跑到楼下
拨了电话又拨他手机才得其门而入
可得其门而入去某个卫生间

我撒了一泡尿出来转了几个房间
却再也找不到刚才进来的门

我想起有一次在大街上的偶遇
他和妻子刚刚跨出宝马
他拦住正好从宝马旁边经过的我
说要向妻子介绍一位诗人
可是那女人晨雾般的眼眸
拂过我的脸面继而便去注视起
我身后那花哨的垃圾筒
直到两分钟后我和他匆匆别过

一个男人就这么死了
想起这些
我真的忍不住要写一首诗

A Man Died

a man died

a man with stunning looks

who one day riding on a motor-cycle taxi

had his head crashing into a beautiful lamp

post newly buried by the side of the street

a man died

it's not important

why he went riding a motor-cycle taxi on an impulse

even though he owned a hegemonic blue BMW

it is important, though, that, apart from the BMW

he had two four-room houses, each with a sitting-room

and he also had a wife so pretty she'd set one's desires on fire

thinking of a bed immediately

I remember once pressing the bell on his door

for 302 in unit 1 but he was 303 in unit 2

I then ran downstairs

calling him on the landline, then his mobile phone, before I could get in

then I went into a toilet

where I pissed and when I came out, through a few rooms

I could not find the door by which I had come in

I remember once meeting them

as the man and his wife had just got out of their BMW

he stopped me as I was about to go past their BMW

saying he wanted to introduce me to his wife as a poet

but the woman's morning-fog eyes

swept past my face to dwell on

the florid rubbish bin behind me

till I said bye in a hurry two minutes subsequently

a man died just like that

remembering all those things

I can't help writing this poem

一个跑向洗手间的妓女

妓女跑向洗手间
她已经接连做了两笔生意
所以她必须跑得快些再快些

妓女在两个老嫖客色迷迷的桃花眼里奔跑
在两个老嫖客色迷迷的桃花眼里
跑向洗手间的妓女
她仅仅只是乐死人的一只剧烈摇摆的丰腴的
屁股

妓女来不及关门就在抽水马桶上蹲下
她撒了一泡无关紧要的尿
她还要蹲上三分钟——

妓女一手捏着八张卫生纸
一手摁着肥肥的小腹
她看到下边的断崖上那些日渐枯黄凋零的茅草
忍不住就心疼地想起了家乡山坡地里
那些被日夜盗伐的竹林

继续向下

妓女看到自己那看不见的部位

她的眼前立刻浮现起了中午的电视剧

那个共军被日本兵用刺刀刺了十多刀的那条大腿

那条可怜的大腿上的那个血肉模糊的

伤口

A Prostitute Who Ran Into a Toilet

a prostitute ran into a toilet

she's taken two clients

which meant she had to run faster

the prostitute was running in the peach-flower eyes of the two leery old

     men

and in the peach-flower eyes of the two leery old men

the prostitute who was running towards the toilet

was a mere plumpness of bums, swaying acutely

that pleasurised one to death

before she had time to close the door the prostitute squatted over the bowl

she pissed an unimportant piss

and she had three more minutes to squat—

eight tissues in one hand

and the other hand pressing down on her fat lower abdomen

the prostitute saw the daily decaying cogon grass on the broken cliff

and she couldn't help thinking, with pain at heart, of the bamboo forest

that got cut by stealth day and night on the slope at her home

and, going down further

she saw her invisible parts

as the TV drama came to her eye that she had watched at noon

with the communist soldier's thigh bayoneted more than 10 times by the

    Japs

the pitiful thigh carrying a cut

smeared with blood

交流

在酒吧，我们隔着一张桌子

你说："我作为一个真诚的诗人……"
我低下头，去注意一颗半生不熟的草莓

在酒吧，我们隔着一张桌子

你说："当我面对博大的汉语言……"
我伸出三个手指，悄然捡起了这颗草莓

在酒吧，我们隔着一张桌子

你的小平头很平整，可是丰肥的下巴太油光可鉴
我嚼了一下嘴里的草莓尝到了一股腐烂的异味

在酒吧，我们隔着一张桌子

我忽然想起刚刚读到你的一首诗："在七月，冰凉的火焰
和海洋一起燃烧，我目睹了一场无法窜改的闪电……"

在酒吧，我们隔着一张桌子

默默俯身，我在桌面上吐出一小撮嚼烂了的东西
我想，我把这颗草莓放到嘴里绝对是个错误

Communications

in the bar, we were separated by a table

you said: 'I, as a sincere poet...'
I lowered my head, noticing a strawberry that was half ripe

in the bar, we were separated by a table

you said: 'When I face the great and rich Chinese language...'
I extended three fingers, to quietly pick up this strawberry

in the bar, we were separated by a table

your cropped hair was rather neat but your fat chin was mirror-shining,
       oily
 I chewed the strawberry, tasting its strange ulcer

in the bar, we were separated by a table

I suddenly recalled having read one of your poems, 'In July, the icy fire
was ablaze with the sea as I witnessed a lightning that refused to be
       revised...'

in the bar, we were separated by a table

quietly, I spat out a squash of the chewed stuff on the table

as I thought: it's an absolute mistake putting the strawberry in my mouth

一条鱼和一次爱

一条小小的鱼
它能够活上 500 岁
这是真的——

我们非但听得真切
而且还看到了
它在海里闲逛遨游的样子

那个晚上
当我们摁灭了电视荧屏
紧接着就做起了爱来

完事之后
一面喘息的我们
一面意犹未尽地感慨

你说：
"这么小个鱼
也能活上个 500 年！"

我说：

"而我们还能

做多少次爱……"

Fish and Love

a tiny little fish
can live to 500 years old
for real—

we have not only clearly heard this
we have also seen
how leisurely it was, strolling in the sea

that night
as soon as we switched off the television
we began making love

afterwards
panting, we were sighing
as we were feeling inadequate

you said,
'such a tiny little fish
can live to 500 years!'

I said,

'but we, how many more times can we

make love…'

我为什么要撒尿

在夜间或者中午——
我是说，当我们一起
躺倒在床上睡觉的时候
——我老婆总是习惯
经常把她的手搁在
我的裆部或者是小腹上

于是她也就经常
抓住了我的把柄——
我是说，当一只打盹的鸟
它突然振翅欲飞
或者说是它突然
变成了另外某个物件的时候
——每当这尴尬的一刻
我警觉的老婆她总是
不厌其烦地
嚷嚷着一句话

她说："哎，你干什么？"

而我的对策从来就只有一个
——我总是一骨碌起床
然后不厌其烦地
咕哝着回答——
"干什么？它要撒尿！"

——已经有很多年了
我和老婆都闹不明白
这鸟哪来这么多的尿
尤其是——它怎么落下了
这样一个奇怪的
一沾床就来尿的毛病

Why Did I Want to Piss?

at night, or, at noon—
I mean, when we lie together
asleep in bed
—my wife is used to putting her hand
on my crotch or my lower abdomen

and, so, she frequently
grabs hold of my handle—
I mean, at the moment when a sleeping bird
is taking sudden flight
or when it suddenly
turns into something else
—at such awkward moments
my vigilant wife never tires
of saying, rather noisily

she says, 'Hey, what are you doing?'

and my response is always this
—I always roll quickly out of bed
and mumble, very patiently—
'what am I doing? But it wants to piss!'

—for many years now

neither my wife nor I understand

why the bird contains so much piss

particularly—how it falls

such a strange sick habit

that piss comes the minute it touches the bed

车祸

先是耳鼻，不住地淌血
后来她想开口说
话于是更多的鲜血
从她的口中，涌出……

这是个过分漂亮的女人
哪怕血污狼藉
脸蛋还是这么生动娇媚
而紧身的花格子西装，花格子短裙
而仍然完好无损的青灰色丝袜
而两只黑亮的方头时装鞋，仍然穿在她的脚上
——只是，她那别致的坤包
甩在了三米之外
而她那辆雪白的轻骑，扑跌得，更远

而那猥琐的出租车司机
面无人色地钻出他的红色桑塔纳
慌得只知道，跑去捡那只坤包
一边反复绝望地哀嚎："太快了——
她真的是太快了，我怎么也来不及……"

而当围观的人群还未合拢之前
差点儿也成了主角的我，在街心
陀螺般转了几圈，然后跳过去
惊魂未定地抱起了她——
而我听到了两个互相激烈追逐的心跳
同时闻到了血腥和血腥中的芳香

"我来不及，真的来不及了
……我要给我女儿喂奶，她饿呀……
她哭得好凶呢，她嚷着要我，要吃奶……"
——这是她芬芳的一句话，好像是说给我听的
而这是她留下的最后一句话，如兰吐气中
我目睹了她的粉红色的美丽胸脯——

她鼓胀的胸口无声息地崩落了
紧身花格子西装的，第一枚纽扣……

The Car Accident

first it's the ears and the nose, that kept bleeding
then, when she wanted to open her mouth to talk
more blood
gushed, out of her mouth...

this is an overly-pretty woman
despite the bloody mess
her face remained vividly delicate and charming
her tight-fitting checkered suit, her short checkered skirt
her dark-grey silk socks that remained intact
the square-headed fashion shoes, black and shiny, that her feet still had on
—only her unconventional bag
had been knocked three metres off
and her white motorcycle, lying down, further away

and the cabdriver, looking wretched
all colour gone from his face, crept out of his red Santana
and, in his panic, ran to pick up the bag
as he wailed repeatedly, 'So fast—
she was so fast, I had no time to...'

and before the crowd closed in

I, almost the centre of attention myself, turned around

a few times, right in the middle of the street, when I leaped over

still badly shaken, to hold her in my arms—

and heard two hearts race in a mutual chase

at the same time when I smelt the blood and the fragrance of the blood

'I was in a hurry, really in a hurry

...I meant to suckle my child as she was starving...

she was crying so hard, she cried for me, she wanted milk...'

—these were her last fragrant words, as if all for my ear

and these were her last remaining words, like a breath through the orchid
     flowers

I witnessed her beautiful pink breasts—

the first button burst, soundless, out of her tight-fitting checkered suit on

her swollen breasts...

色情狂

这是个真实的笑话
说笑话的是一个
长了一脸青春痘的护士小姐

笑话里的三个主角
都是 10 号病房的病人
28 床——肾小球发炎的 48 岁的男子
29 床——乳房癌术后不适的 39 岁的妇女
（30 床空位）
31 床——因癌细胞而切除了 8 公分直肠
顺便也切除了肛门的 61 岁的老头

说的是有一天深夜——
28 床的男子，小声对 29 床的妇女
说了一句："你千万不要喊不要叫！"
然后就，爬上了她的床

而螳螂捕蝉，往往是黄雀在后
31 床的老头，行动不便

却神智清醒的老头他及时偷偷
按上了，床头的小按钮……

笑话的高潮也就是结尾部分
大家一定都猜到了——
正在这千钧一发之际，10号病房
气喘吁吁地跑进来一个
长了一脸青春痘的，护士小姐

Sex-Mad

this is a real joke

about a nurse

whose face is covered in acne

three characters in this joke

are all patients in ward 10

bed 28: a man, 48, with infected glomerulus

bed 29: a woman, 39, suffering from discomfiture after a cancer operation

bed 30: an empty bed

bed 31: a man, 61, who shed an 8-cm-long rectum due to cancerous cells
        and had

his anus removed along the way

the story has it that, very late one night

Bed 28 says to Bed 29, in a low voice:

'don't cry or scream!'

as he says it he creeps onto her bed

when a mantis is stalking a cicada, the oriole is often behind their back

likewise, Bed 31, his movements highly restricted

but his head clear enough, presses the button

of the bedside lamp, by stealth

the joke reaches its orgasm when it ends

as you can all guess

at that particular moment, rushing into ward 10

panting, is Miss Nurse

whose face is covered in acne

处决一个词

处决一个词
是由于它恶心非常
这就像，一股令人倾倒的狐臭
它跑到了一个美丽少女的
腋窝下

但处决一个词
这不像处决一股狐臭

处决一股狐臭
可以处决掉狐臭而保存下少女
以及少女的美丽
甚至以及，少女的腋窝

而处决一个词
得先处决掉一本书
得先处决掉一张报纸
得先处决掉一个电视节目

也许，还得先处决掉一个政党
还得先处决掉一个国家
更要命的是，也许还得
先处决掉多少无辜的人民

所以，你可以把一个恶心的词
处决掉一千次一万次
但只能，在你的假想中

Executing a word

a word is executed
because it is really disgusting
like a captivating fox stink
that ran to a pretty girl's
armpits

but executing a word
is definitely not like executing a fox stink

executing a fox stink
could cause it to be executed and the girl to be kept
and her beauty
and even, her armpits

but to execute a word
is to execute a book
to execute a newspaper
to execute a TV program

or, perhaps, you have to first execute a political party
to execute a nation

and, the most lethal of all, you probably have to

execute so many innocent people

and, for this reason, you could execute a disgusting word

a thousand times, ten thousand times

all in your imagination

石榴裙以及石榴

石榴裙——对这种裙子
我一直，心怀敬畏
因为自古相传
令男人们卑躬又屈膝的
就是这种裙子

可刚刚在电视里
看到一个节目，才知道
其实这不是，某种款式的裙子
而仅是泛指那些
红色的裙子，而已

这个天大的误会，让我想起了
去年的石榴——我从没见过
石榴，更从没吃过——
我终于见到并吃到了一次石榴

但是石榴，我要说
原来我垂涎已久的石榴

它竟然是，那么一种
一点滋味儿也没有的东西

The Pomegranate Skirt and the Pomegranate

the pomegranate skirt—of this kind of skirt
I have always been in awe
because it is this kind of skirt, carried down the ages
that has reduced the male to bent knees

but, from a program I watched
just now on TV, I got to know
that it was not a skirt of a particular style
but a general reference to those
red skirts, merely

this sky-big mistake reminds me
of the pomegranate last year—I had never seen
a pomegranate, let alone eaten one—
that I ended up seeing and eating, for once

but the pomegranate, I must say
the one that I had long been drooling for

turned out to be something

that was so tasteless

诚实的诗人，贞洁的女人

那是初夏黄昏的暖洋洋的大街
我们又一次相遇，互相露出了笑脸

然而你穿着怪模怪样的白衬衣白短裙
然而我听见了自己的心跳感觉到了浑身血液的奔涌

然而我打量着你的别致刺亮的红腰带
然而我说：你真的很漂亮很性感……

然而你立即厌恶地扭转了身
然而你说：讨厌死了！你真恶心……

整个夏天，你都在避免与我相遇
整个夏天，每一次相遇你都在避免与我发生交谈

——我想，我是诚实的，而你是贞洁的
我的诚实让我愧疚，而你的贞洁让我从此辨不清风向

The Honest Poet, the Chaste Woman

it was in that warm street at an early summer dusk
that we met again, with a smile for each other

although you wore a weird blouse and a short skirt
although I heard my heart leap, with a rush of surging blood

although I sized up your red belt, unique and shiny with barbs
although I said: You really are so pretty and sexy...

although you at once turned around, in disgust
although you said: So annoying! You are so disgusting...

all summer, you were trying to avoid me
all summer, whenever we met you tried to avoid talking to me

—I think I am honest and you are chaste
my honesty shaming me and your chastity making me lose a sense of
    direction

细节：鸟窝

电梯里　我年轻的鸟
按捺不住雀跃起来

荒唐的是　与我同梯的
她是个　半老的徐娘

我把双手插入裤袋
我在暗骂她　浑身上下的鬼气息

我把双手攥成拳头
我在暗骂她　那副左转右转的鬼身材

当拳头也无济于事时　我只好
弓起身子　把屁股坐到梯壁的扶手上

电梯升到了 18 层　扭腰出去时她那双鬼眸
仔细地瞥了瞥　我那要命的不断膨胀的鸟窝

电梯继续上升　盯着对面的大框镜
我看见一个欲盖弥彰的男人

这男人沮丧不堪　　他从裤袋里拔出了双手
但是　　他按捺不住的鸟　　已经振翅欲飞了

Detail: Bird's Nest

in the lift   my young bird
could hardly suppress its jump

the absurdity was   she in the same lift
was a half-old   woman

hands inserted in my pants pockets, I
muttered a curse: she generated a devilish air from head to toe

my hands rolled into fists
I muttered: she had a devilish body that turned this way and that

when even my fists failed   I had to
bend double   putting my buttocks on the railings in the lift

as it ascended to Level 18   she twisted her body on the way out her
      devilish eyes
took a careful glance   at my fatal bird's nest that kept expanding

the lift kept ascending   staring at the large-framed mirror facing me I
saw a man trying hard to conceal   only to reveal more

this man was so dejected   he pulled his hands out of his pockets

by then   the irrepressible bird   was a-wing

细节：厌恶

他们　在十字街口
狭路相逢

不约而同地　他们
用极度厌恶的眼神
对视了　两秒种
然后错身　而过

他的耳根　带着
昨夜里　她的猩红唇印

她的体内　带着
昨夜里　他的黏稠欲液

Detail: Disgust

they   narrowly missed
at a crossroads

when   almost at the same time their
eyes locked   for two seconds
in total disgust
before their bodies went past each   other

his earlobe   still printed
with her scarlet lip from   last night

her body   carrying
his sticky liquid as well

细节：反光

飞机冲上云层的一瞬
我看见了　太阳的反光
它来自窗外的机翼
来自机翼上　一枚
小小的　螺丝帽

螺丝帽上的油漆剥落了
所以露出了锃亮的螺丝帽

整整十年了
我是个　每天都与螺丝
打交道的人
根据经验我知道　这枚已经
退出了一小圈螺纹的
锃亮的螺丝
它几乎是　彻底松动了

Detail: Reflection

in the instant in which the plane shoved into the clouds

I saw   the reflection of the sun

coming from a tiny screw

cap on   the wing outside the

window   the wing

the paint peeled on the cap

revealing its shininess

for a full ten years

I was someone   who had been dealing with screws

on a daily basis

and as far as I knew from my experience   this

shining screw

that had come out by a single coil

came almost   thoroughly loose

我在干什么

一个新认识的女诗人
给我打了三次长途电话

第一次是有一天晚饭后
根据老婆指示
我洗刷完一遍浴缸接着
正仔细洗刷抽水马桶

她说："你在干什么？"
我说："写诗。"
她说："什么诗？"
我说："一首关于抽水马桶的诗。"

第二次是有一天晚上
老婆在浴室里
洗她怎么洗也洗不完的衣服
我在客厅看港剧抱儿子
小子他一泡热尿淋湿了我的裤裆
最后尿液顺我的大腿
滴到了地板上

她说："你在干什么？"

我说："写诗。"

她说："什么诗？"

我说："一首写给儿子杨渡的诗。"

第三次是有一天深夜

我和老婆 11 点 35 分上床

到 12 点 10 分各自去上了趟卫生间

准备开始正式睡觉

女诗人的口音在深夜里特别清晰

她说："你现在在干什么？"

我刚躺下合上眼又得爬起身

我说："正写了一首诗。"

女诗人总是饶有兴趣

她说："什么样的诗？"

我想了想

我说："一首献给老婆的诗。"

女诗人停顿了一下

她说："你们结婚已经多少年了？"

我说："表面上是三年实际上是八年。"

她说："这首诗写得长吗？"

我说："是首长诗。"

女诗人又停顿了一下

她说："多少行？"

我又想了想

我说："没数数，应该是三四百来行吧。"

不知为什么那个女诗人从此

再也没给我打第四次长途电话了

What Am I Doing?

a woman poet that I had newly become acquainted with
had made me three long-distance phone calls

the first one after dinner
when, based on my wife's instructions
I had just scrubbed clean the bathtub
and was carefully brushing the toilet bowl

she said, 'What are you doing?'
I said, 'Writing a poem.'
she said, 'What poem?'
I said, 'A poem about the toilet bowl.'

the second came one night
when my wife was in the washroom
doing the laundry that never finished
I, holding my son in my arms, watched a Hong Kong TV drama in the
        sitting room
this bloke pissed, his hot piss drenching my crotch
running down my legs
dripping onto the floor

she said, 'What are you doing?'

I said, 'Writing a poem.'

she said, 'What poem?'

I said, 'A poem to my son, Yang Du.'

the third call came in the middle of a night

when we began to officially go to sleep

after my wife and I went to bed at 11.35pm

and each of us went to the loo, separately, at 12.10am

the woman poet's voice was particularly distinct late at night

she said, 'What are you doing now?'

I had just lain down in bed and closed my eyes when I had to get out of bed

    again

I said, 'I've just written a poem.'

the woman poet was always interested

she said, 'What sort of a poem?'

I gave it a thought

I said, 'A poem dedicated to my wife.'

there was a pause

she said, 'How many years have you been married?'

I said, 'Three years but actually eight.'

she said, 'Is it a long poem?'

I said, 'A long one.'

there was another pause

she said, 'How many lines?'

I gave it another thought

and said, 'I haven't counted it. Should be about three to four hundred lines.'

for some reason, the woman poet has

never made me another long-distance call again

我们每个人都是不折不扣的天才

显而易见他俩是来自外地的民工
——在购物中心广场的
大花坛边，他俩显而易见正在
因为感情问题而纠缠

她应该是在哭诉着什么
嘴里飞快喷发着古怪的方言
大颗大颗眼泪簌簌地滴落
还有吸溜得响亮的鼻涕，还有
不顾一切夸张甩动的手臂……

他应该是在挽回着什么
小声地，怯懦地，一边不停
用双手去拢她甩动的手臂
然而就那么几分钟
就那么几分钟时间
她开始破涕为笑了——
先是拉着手，随后是搂着腰肩
他俩就转而朝广场外走去
在黄昏来临的那一刻

可爱的民工，可爱的狠狠拌了
一回嘴的准小两口（应该是吧）
我不知道，当他俩回到自己的住处
（某栋居民楼底下的储物室
或者是这城市的哪一个角落）
今晚是否还能够开心地做爱
然而有一个结论我已经确信无疑
——其实生活中，我们每个人
常常都是不折不扣的天才

We, All of Us, Are Out-and-Out Geniuses

it's obvious that they two are peasant workers from outside this city
—at the flower beds

in the shopping plaza, they obviously are entangled
with something emotional

she is probably crying over something
her strange broad accent fast tumbling out of her mouth
large drops of tears dripping
a noisy sniffing nose, and
her arms brandishing in an exaggerated manner...

he must have been trying to save the situation
talking in a low voice, timidly, while stopping
to hold her brandishing arms with his hands
and it only took a few minutes
and in those few minutes

she began choking back her tears—
they went away, first hand in hand, then holding each other around the
        back
turning around and walking towards the edge of the plaza
in the instant when dusk fell

these lovely peasant workers, lovely (must-be) quasi-couple

who had a tough argument

I do not know if they are able to make happy love tonight

when they go back to where they live

(a storeroom at the bottom of a residential building

or a corner in this city)

although I am certain

—each and every one of us, in real life

are out-and-out geniuses

邻居的幽默

邻居正在门口数钱
他的钱来自
一个面色苍白的小姑娘
小姑娘瞥一眼他那哆嗦的双手
转身傲然下楼而去

见我开门出来
邻居干笑了笑解释说
最近他家楼下那晦暗的储物室
已经出租给刚才那位外地小姐
做了卧室

人到中年的邻居
幽默的中学物理教师
把那几张人民币递到了我眼皮下
他说你看看这血汗钱哪
多么的汗津津

My Neighbour's Humour

my neighbour was counting his money

his money that came

from a pale-faced girl

the little girl glanced at his quivering hands

before she turned and walked away downstairs, proudly

seeing me open the door and come out

my neighbour, with a dry laugh, explained

that his dark storeroom downstairs

had been rented to the *xiaojie* from somewhere else

as her bedroom

my neighbour, middle-aged

was a humorous physics teacher at a middle school

he thrust the number of RMB notes under my nose

and said: Look at this blood and sweat money

isn't it sweaty

一本被我读得破旧不堪的书

一本被我读得破旧不堪的书
也就是一本被我反复蹂躏的书
当然，它经受不了我的蹂躏
它身上留下了许多
被我蹂躏的痕迹
因此它变得，破旧不堪

一本被我读得破旧不堪的书
它记录了我的暴行
我必须掩饰，我的不道德
它将泄露关于我的某些信息
我必须封锁，一切秘而不宣

一本被我读得破旧不堪的书
它不得不从我的堂皇书架，离开
被我层层打包
然后锁进黑暗的书橱
成为我的，一个小小的隐私

A Book Much Worn Down With My Reading

a book much worn down with my reading

e.g. one that was repeatedly ravaged by me

of course, it couldn't stand my ravaging

its body covered with multiple traces

of my ravaging

so much so that it has become   old and used

a book so old and used with my reading

it's a record of my violence

I have to cover up   my immorality

it'll leak some of my information

I have to blockade it   have to be secretive

a book so old and used with my reading

it has to leave   my glorious bookshelf

to be wrapped up layer after layer by me

before it is locked away in a dark bookcase

as my   little private self

什么正在离开之中

夜半梦醒
探身靠在床头
我分明听见什么
它正在，离开
隐隐发出了滴答
滴答的声响

我屏声倾听
分辨出，这声音似乎
来自隔壁的浴室

哦，是洗手盆上的那个水龙头
——很小很小的一滴
——很慢很慢的一滴
它突然坏了
它在滴水
一直在滴水

从浴室里出来
回到床上，重新靠在床头

——我又分明听见
什么，它正在离开
隐隐发出了滴滴答答
滴滴答答的声响

我屏声倾听
分辨出这声音，似乎
不仅仅来自隔壁的浴室

哦，我终于明白了
不仅仅是洗手盆上的
那个水龙头坏了
其实还有另外的一个
水龙头——
它也坏了，它在滴水
一直，在滴水

滴答
滴答
滴答

没错，最后我找到那声音了
——那声音好像

就来自
我的，体内

Something Is Taking Leave

midnight, when I woke up from a dream

and leaned against the head of my bed

I clearly heard something

taking leave, leaving

while faintly ticking

with sounds of ticking

I held my breath and listened

I could make out that the sound seemed

coming from the bathroom next door

ah, it's the tap over the washing basin

—a tiny little drop

—a very slow drop

it suddenly went kaput

it was dripping

had been dripping

coming out of the bathroom

and returning to my bed, I leaned against the head of the bed

—but again clearly heard
something, taking leave
faintly ticking
with sounds of ticking

I held my breath and listened
making out that the sound, seemed
not just coming from the bathroom next door

oh, I realised
that it was not just the tap over the washing basin
that went kaput
there was actually another
tap—also gone kaput, and was dripping
had been, dripping,

tick tacking
tick tocking
tick tacking

right. I finally located the sound

—the sound that seemed

issuing from

my, body

儿子和小雪人

小雪人很矮，然而
一岁半的儿子要更矮一些
他迈着稚气的小脚步
靠近小雪人，好奇地去碰碰
小雪人的胳臂和肩膀

儿子用小手，指了指
飘着一朵朵大雪片儿的天空
又指指身边的小雪人
小嘴里发出快乐的嘻笑
然后，儿子又用小手去拍拍
小雪人的额头和脸蛋
一边含糊地，呼唤着什么

雪地里的儿子，他的
小脸蛋儿，是红扑扑的
可无论怎么拍打呼唤
我知道，这小雪人
小脸蛋儿雪白雪白的小雪人
是决不会，应答出声的了

——但是几分钟后
奇迹，出现了——
在儿子的欢呼中，我看到
小雪人突然撒出了
一泡，长长的热尿

热气腾腾的一泡热尿
冲开了结实的雪身——
倏忽间，小雪人
有了完整的，屁股蛋儿
还有两条，可爱的小腿儿……

Son and the Little Snowman

the little snowman is short although
my son, a year and a half old, is shorter
he walks in small, young steps
up to the little snowman, touching the arm and the shoulder of
the snowman out of curiosity

my son points with his little hand
at the sky with large snowflakes
he points at the little snowman by his side
a happy giggle issuing from his little mouth
then, with his little hand, he pats
the forehead and face of the little snowman
calling out for something, confusedly

my son in the snow, his
little face flushed red
however hard he pats or cries
I know, the little snowman
with a small white face
won't make a response
—however, a few minutes later
a miracle happens—
amidst my son's cheers, I see

the little snowman suddenly shoot

out, a long hot piss

a steaming hot piss

that rushes out of an opening in the solid snow body—

all of a sudden, the little snowman

has complete, buttocks

and two, lovely little legs...

女诗人

她的名字很美，并且是
大家所熟悉的——
在一个有多位诗人聚集的场合
我们不知怎么谈起了她

照片里的她特别漂亮
但我听说，这些都是以前的
"如果见到她，你一定觉得她
已经不那么漂亮了——
可如今，她的裤腰带儿
还是像以前那么的松……"

这些男诗人，似乎都像熟悉
她的名字一样熟悉她的生活习惯
"如果你和她有了一手
那好，明儿个走上大街
你就多了一大帮亲戚……"
——这些可恶的男诗人，他们
每说一句话都这样含蓄而风趣

"但她的诗真的好，真的没说的
——永远和她从前一样漂亮！"
我侧耳听着他们诸如此类
不肯轻易出口的，赞美之词
倏忽间，竟然莫名其妙地
对一位从未谋面的女诗人
有了某种，异常亲切的感觉

该死的莫名其妙的感觉
大半年过去了，居然还能
让我在今天下午，让我在
一本刚出刊的杂志上
异常亲切地读起了女诗人的诗
——这些短诗，真是没说的
结构松垮（好像传说中
她的那条，裤腰带儿？）
诗句急促而凌厉，直接而漂亮
在这无聊的下午，它们
让我感动并为此要写一首诗

The Woman Poet

she had a beautiful name, one that was
familiar to all—
on one occasion when many a poet gathered
we somehow started talking about her

in her photograph, she was especially pretty
although I heard that was many years ago
'if you see her, I am sure you'll find her
not that pretty any more—'
still, her waist belt
was as loose as ever before...

these male poets seemed as familiar
with her name as with her living habits
'if you lay your hands on her
that'll be good because when you go out tomorrow
you'll be plus a large group of relatives...'
these disgusting male poets, every word they said
was so subtle and salty

'but it goes without saying that her poetry is really good
—always as pretty as she was before!'
listening, with half an ear, to such

praise that wouldn't easily come out of their mouths

I suddenly developed, without knowing why

an exceptionally familiar feeling

towards a woman poet I had never met

damn! This weird feeling

more than six months ago, was such

it enabled me to read her poems with an exceptional intimacy

on an issue of a magazine, just published

that afternoon

—these short poems, it goes without saying

had a loose structure (just like the legend

about her waist belt?)

the lines were rapid and forceful, direct and pretty

on this boring afternoon, they

moved me so much that I wanted to write this poem because of it

忽然就下起雨来

先是小雨点
稀稀拉拉落下来

我看见
十字街口的电话亭里
一个头发蓬乱衣衫不整的女人
倚着不锈钢管坐在
那张小小的大理石地面上

当我走近了一点
我看见了
她的袒胸露乳
噢——可怜的女人
可怜的一个神智不清的女人

此时电话亭背后转出
一个嬉笑着的小孩
他跑过来跪下
在女人怀里吸了一口奶
又嬉笑着跑出去

当我再走近了一点
我看清楚了女人的衣着
她的眼神和笑脸
哦——这不是个神智不清的女人
她应该是来自外地的民工

这女人也许是带着孩子逛街
因为忽然下起雨来
她才进了电话亭避雨
一边看着街景
顺便一边给她的孩子喂奶

当我走到电话亭旁时
我看见这嬉笑着的小孩
他又绕过来跑进电话亭
又过去跪下双腿
趴在女人怀里吸奶

这小孩敏捷的动作告诉我
他应该是比我那一岁半的儿子
早出生几个月的
可他黑不溜秋脏里吧叽且瘦得厉害
他的个儿比我儿子要矮许多

我清楚看见了母亲怀里的
那两只黄褐色的空荡荡垂着的口袋
而她的儿子捧着它们快乐地嬉笑
一会儿在左边的乳房吸几口
一会儿又在右边的乳房吸几口

母亲默默无声地呵笑着
她干脆把内衣高高掀起
然后用双手去抚摩她的儿子
一只放在他的头顶
一只放在不住摇摆的黑屁股蛋

嘿——袒胸露乳的母亲
她也许奶惯了孩子
她无所顾忌也许是因为在她的眼里
这儿的热闹大街与她老家
山旮旯里静悄悄的院子毫无区别

唉——当我看着这一幕
作为一个年过三十的男人
作为一个年迈母亲的儿子
和一个一岁半儿子的父亲
我忽然心头发热两眼闪出了泪花

街上的小雨点变成了大点大点的雨
同时这雨点越来越稠密起来
以至人们在街上慌忙逃窜
而没有打伞的我慢慢沿街边走着
仰头让雨点任意拍打我的脸面

嗬——久不下雨的天空
忽然就下起这样一场痛快的雨来

All of a Sudden, It Rained

first, it was little raindrops
that fell, sparsely

when I saw
in a phone booth at the crossroads
a woman, disheveled and slipshod
sitting on the small square of the granite floor
against the stainless steel pipe

as I got close
I could see
her exposed breasts
oh—a pitiable woman
a pitiable woman out of her senses

just then, a grinning kid
came in running from behind the booth
to kneel
and suckle the woman's breasts
before he, grinning, went out again

when I got closer
I could see her clothes

the way she looked and her smiling face
oh, no, it's not a woman out of her senses
she must be a peasant worker from elsewhere

she may have been window-shopping with her kid
and have come into the booth to avoid
the sudden rain
watching the street scene
as she was breastfeeding her kid

by the time I had got to the booth
I could see the grinning kid
running around into it again
to kneel before the woman
and suck on her breasts

the quick acts of the boy told me
that he must have been born a few months earlier
than my 18-month-old son
but he was dark, dirty and thin
much shorter than my son, too

clearly, I could see the two brown sags, hanging empty
in his mother's bosom
and her son, holding them, with a happy grin
sucking on her left for a second

before he sucked on the other one

his mother ha-haed
she simply lifted her underclothes
caressing her son's head with both her hands
one on the top of his head
and the other, on his swaying black bum

ah, well—a mother with open breasts
she may have habitually suckled her kid thus
she had no scruples perhaps because in her eyes
this busy street was no different
from the quiet courtyard in her old home in the depths of the mountain

well, then—when I saw that
my heart burnt and tears came to my eyes
as a man who had gone past 30
the son of an ageing mother
and the father of an 18-month-old boy

the little raindrops over the street became bigger
and denser, so much so
that people started running around on the street
as I, without an umbrella, took my time strolling
my head raised to let the raindrops pat me on the face

wow—the sky that had stayed rainless for a long time

was coming down with such a joyful rain

浅薄的男人

有一次，我曾经在几个朋友中间
绘声绘色地讲述了自己
险些遭受的一场车祸——
我指着我们正行走着的那条街道
我说，那天晚上下着蒙蒙小雨
我骑着自行车，就在这一段
我与一辆摩托车相遇
我骑得很快，可迎面而来的摩托车更快
我与对方交错而过的刹那
我才发现，那不是一辆摩托车
我太想当然了
我以为那盏刺眼的车灯是摩托车的
我没料到的是，那是一辆小货车
我看到的是右大灯
我看不到左大灯，因为它是不亮的
我幸亏与心目中的摩托车保持了距离
我选择的那么一点儿距离，刚刚好
我没有夸张，只是有点煽情
我说这刚好是一辆小货车的宽度也是
我与死亡之间的精确距离

我如果再偏过去一公分那么

我肯定马上就会飞起来

我飞起来划了个弧

我的身体啪嗒落下的那一刻

我想我就看到马克思了

我啧舌说

我幸亏没有偏过去一公分

我与小货车擦身而过时

我其实已来不及躲避

我感觉小货车的车头和车厢飞快擦过

我的手腕我的膝盖和

我的衬衣的下摆，但就是刚刚好

我没有受到那种巨大力量的撞击，所以

我的性命没有被那个天杀的司机剥夺，所以现在

我还存在于这个人类的世界……

——我讲述到了最后部分

才注意到了大家的表情，我才醒悟

他们根本没有被我的讲述所吸引——

他们当中，只有一个朋友

在与我四目对接的当儿，对我

露出了敷衍的微笑，而另有一个

脸上带着一丝牵强的惊悸

但在我进行末尾的总结时他的眼睛直了

他的脖子被什么牵引得拉长了许多
——循着他直愣愣的目光，我看到
前面的十字街口，刚好闪过了一个女人的一只
风情满溢的屁股……

那个阳光强烈的下午，后来
我们在那条街道上接着又走了
一段不短的路——
而我硬生生地咽下了最后一个
语气词，再也没有言语
——我感到自己的喉咙在刺痛
同时，作为一个年过三十的男人
我为自己刚才的浅薄
感到了难以言表的愧疚——
借着拍去脸上一只飞蝇的机会
我狠狠扇了自己，一个响亮的耳光

The Shallow Man

once, when I was with a few friends of mine

I vividly described a car accident

that nearly killed myself—

pointing to the street we were walking on

I said that it was drizzling that night

and I was riding a bike, right at this section

when I encountered a motorcycle

I was riding fast but the oncoming motorcycle was faster

it was not till the instant in which I went past it

that I realised that it was not a motorcycle

that I had wrongly assumed it was

I had thought that the blinding headlights were from a motorcycle

I had not expected that it was a mini-truck

I saw the right headlight

I could not see the left headlight because it was not on

fortunately, I kept a distance from my mental motorcycle

the distance I had chosen was, just about right

I did not exaggerate, I was only being sensational

I said that it was just the width of the truck also the exact distance

between death and I

if I had been one centimetre further that way

I would have been flown up

and I would have drawn a curve in my flight

and in the instant in which my body crash landed

I would have met Karl Marx

I clucked my tongue and said

I was lucky not to have gone the other way by one more centimetre

when I scraped with the truck

I had in fact no time to dodge it

I felt that the head of the truck and its body flew past

my wrist my knee and

the lower edge of my shirt but only just

I was not hit with the huge impact, which is why

my life remains intact from the heaven-should-kill driver, which is why

I still exist in this human world...

—it was not till I reached the final part

when I took note of their facial expressions, that I realised

that they were not at all attracted by my description—

among them, only one friend

smiled reluctantly to me

when our eyes connected, and another one

had a look of astonishment that was slightly stretched

but his eyes went blank when I summed it all up

his neck lengthened as if pulled by something

—along the way his dazed eye looked, I saw

the lush buttocks of a woman

who had just flashed across the crossroads ahead of us...

that afternoon of strong sunlight, and later

we walked quite a long distance

on that street—

when I swallowed hard the last

modal particle, no more words left

—I felt my throat ached

and, at the same time, as a male who had gone past 30

I felt an inexpressible sense of guilt

about my shallowness—

I slapped myself hard and loud

by taking the opportunity to slap at a fly on my face

孩子

她七岁，刚读小学一年级
个子矮小，黑瘦
而开学前一天她把脑袋后面的
独角辫剪掉了，要做个男孩

每天上学，爸爸骑五分钟自行车
带她到离家最近的公交车亭
然后她独自坐公交车上学
放学时，爸爸就在那个公交车亭候着

有一天在公交车亭，爸爸多候了
半个多钟头，天都快黑了
结果才在焦急万分之中
等到了匆匆独行而来的她

爸爸大发雷霆，而她说出了原委
——可能是不小心弄丢了
她怎么也没找到今天的另一个硬币
因此循着行车的路线，她一步步走了回来

孩子的口气和神情始终是那么平静
虽然她的眼窝里，牢牢钉着两颗泪
而息怒后的爸爸突然想号啕大哭
虽然，爸爸咬牙顶住了所有的闸门

爸爸想，这孩子多么像他自己
可有什么还能比这更值得自豪的呢
噢——爸爸轻轻吐出了一个叹词
后来只是，伸手摸了又摸孩子的后脑勺

The Kid

she was seven and was studying at Grade 1, in a primary school
she was short, small, dark and thin
and, the day before the school opening, she had had her single horn-like
      pigtail
behind her cut as she wanted to be a boy

every day at school time, her dad would ride his bike for five minutes
taking her to the bus stop, nearest to her home
and, alone, she would take the bus to school
after school, her dad would wait at the bus stop

one day, at the bus stop, her dad had waited for more than
half an hour, and it was not till the day was getting dark
when he was getting exceedingly worried
that she came alone, hurrying

her dad stormed and she explained
—perhaps out of carelessness, she had lost
another coin that she couldn't find however hard she tried
so she retraced her footsteps along the bus route, step by step

the kid spoke and looked so calm, from beginning to end
although two drops of tears were firmly nailed in her eyes

and her dad, whose fury had died down, felt like bursting into tears

still, he clenched his teeth against all the sluicegates

he thought to himself how much the kid resembled himself

and what was there that he should be more proud of

ah, well—her dad breathed out a gentle interjection

and ended up, touching the back of his kid's head, with his hand

割草机

它们发出呜呜的吼叫，仿佛在地底
低沉而持续地震撼着楼上
我的，几乎搁浅的午睡

我走到窗边，愠怒地俯视深深的下面
哦——原来是它们，四只怪兽
匍匐在，生机勃勃的草坪

它们排着队，它们前进的步伐整齐
它们欢快地吞噬着嫩叶
它们发出的声音恐怖，让人惊悸

The Lawnmower

they roared in a low voice, as if from the bottom of the earth

shaking my siesta, nearly stranded, upstairs

in a deepening and continuous way

I went to the window, resentfully, looking deep down

oh, I see, it's them, four strange animals

crawling, over the lively lawn

they lined up, they advanced in neat unison

and they happily swallowed tender leaves

the noise they issued terrifying, horrifying even

比喻

我做过许多年煤气热水器的修理工
——有一次在修理部里，我拆开了
一台热水器的上壳
它的主人——送它来检修的顾客
打扮时尚的年轻女人
携着她七八岁的宝贝女儿
在我身旁，观看着我的现场维修

卸下了彩色上壳的热水器，再没有
花哨的商标和装饰了——
裸露着铜质与钢质零部件
以及塑料配件，凌乱的导线等等
它们只讲究实用有效，却忽略了美观

"哇！妈妈，这热水器里面
怎么会是这样难看的呢？"
——洋娃娃般的宝贝女儿惊讶了
而漂亮妈妈微微启齿一笑——
"对呀，这就好像是我们的身体一样
脱掉了衣服，不也是很难看的嘛……"

——多么突兀却又自然而然

宝贝女儿把目光从壁头的热水器，移到了

漂亮妈妈身上，停留了两秒钟

"噢……"她小嘴里轻轻发出了

一个叹词，目光又落回到她们家的热水器上

宝贝女儿和漂亮妈妈不会知道

那么多年过去了，当年那个技术高超而

如今早已洗手不干了的师傅

他一直完完整整记着那一刻

那一刻所有动人的细节以及，那个关键的比喻

A Metaphor

I have worked as a repairer of gas hot water services for many years
—once, in the repair shop, I dismantled
the upper case of a service
its owner—a client who had brought it in for maintenance
a young woman, quite fashionably dressed
was by my side, with her cherished daughter, aged 7 or 8
watching me repair it on site

the service, after the colour upper case was removed, had
no florid trademark or decoration—
it was naked with spare parts of copper or steel
or plastic, as well as a mess of wiring
very practical in their ignorance of appearance

'wow, Mom, why does the inside look so ugly?'
—the doll-like daughter was surprised
and her pretty mom grinned—
'that's right. It's like our body
that looks ugly when undressed...'

—so abrupt and so natural
her treasured daughter moved her eye from the service to
her pretty mom, stopping for two seconds

'oh,…' her tiny mouth gently
interjected, as her eye fell back on their hot water service

neither the daughter nor her pretty mom knew
that, many years after, the master technician, with superb skills
has washed his hands of this
but still remembers that particular moment
with all its moving details and, that key metaphor

黑白分明

今天，我从没这样
怀疑过白和黑

我坐在白天里
——我觉得这样的白非常可疑

是不是有人故意破坏了时间
是不是因为有太多的人，阴谋把黑说成了白

我坐在黑夜里
——我觉得这样的黑非常可疑

是不是有人故意破坏了时间
是不是因为有太多的人，合力把白说成了黑

我从没这样，怀疑过白和黑
在今天

Black and White

it's not till today
that I've wondered so much about black and white

I sit in the white day
—I find such whiteness very suspicious

is there anyone who has deliberately destroyed time
or are there too many who conspire to say black is white

I sit in the dark night
—I find such darkness very questionable

is there anyone who has deliberately destroyed time
or are there too many who, in a common effort, say that white is black

it's not till today
that I've had so much doubt about black and white

溃烂

一只梨和一只苹果，肩并着肩
——在书桌一角的托盘上
它俩，差不多等我一个多星期了

一只梨和一只苹果，肩并着肩
我天天对着它俩——看光线在不同质地的
皮表上反复抚摩，看阴影在周围

时刻发生着，小小的变幻
——而直到有一天我察觉到苹果上
长出了一颗青春痘般大小的，可疑花斑

我找来水果刀，移过托盘——
这才赫然发现问题不是苹果，反倒是
这只梨的那一面，早就已经烂了个指甲盖大的疤……

——把烂梨送往厨房，丢进垃圾桶
然后削掉小花斑以及全部的苹果皮
接着一分为二，我切开了洁白无瑕的苹果

这是多么触目惊心——我目睹了两瓣洁白
严严实实包裹着两个，让人恶心反胃
让人毛骨悚然的，偷偷溃烂的世界……

Rotting

a pear and an apple, shoulder to shoulder
—on a plate in a corner of my desk
they both, had been awaiting me for over a week

a pear and an apple, shoulder to shoulder
I faced them daily—to see the light repeating its massage
over the skin, differently textured, and to see the surrounding shadows

constantly presenting, tiny changes
—till one day when I sensed the apple
growing a puberty pimple, a suspect flower spot

I found a fruit knife, moving the plate over—
when I suddenly realised that the problem was not the apple but
the pear whose other side had rotten till a fingernail-sized scar appeared...

—I took the rotten pear to the kitchen and chucked it into the bin
I then sliced off the little flower spot and peeled the whole apple
halving it, I opened the purely white, spotless apple

how shocking—I witnessed the two white halves
tightly wrapping up the two, stomach-turning
hair-raising, worlds that were secretly rotting away...

如何处理垃圾

必须把果皮纸屑包装袋之类等等的垃圾

放进垃圾桶

——这个常识

是在儿子刚学会走路那会儿

我就教给他了的

不到两岁的儿子

在我教了两次之后

他就养成了

凡是垃圾都要往垃圾桶里送的

好习惯

可每当在户外

牢记常识的儿子

总是为找不到垃圾箱或垃圾筒而着急

他的小手里紧紧握着什么

作为父母的我们

也跟着他一起团团转

——为了垃圾以及垃圾箱或垃圾筒

我们变得越来越神经质

而与此同时

渐渐长大的儿子具备了
观察和独立思考的能力
——几乎每一天
他总要固执地发出疑问
他说爸爸或者说妈妈
那为什么大人们
他们都乱扔垃圾呢

是啊这些太不讲文明的大人们
这些太不讲卫生的大人们
这些太不自爱太不热爱环境的大人们
这些不知羞耻的大人们哪
这些不要脸的大人们哪
——都忍了四年了
这一天再也忍不住了
我对儿子发狠说
从今天开始你就可以乱扔垃圾了
像这些大人们一样
而儿子很疑惑
儿子说为什么呢
我说不为什么就因为你也是大人了
而吃完冰棍的儿子疑惑地
把手中的小棒儿丢到地上时

顺便还有模有样

朝地上吐了口唾沫

我咬咬牙

向已经六岁了的儿子竖起大拇指

我说儿子你对了

以后在外面哪

就得这么干

How to Deal With Rubbish

one must bin

all sorts of rubbish like fruit peels shredded paper and packing bags

—this common sense

I had taught my son

just as he was beginning to learn how to walk

my son, aged less than two

after I taught him twice

had formed a good habit

of binning any rubbish

still, once outdoors

my son, keeping the common sense firmly in mind

got worried for not being able to find a bin

his little hand tightly holding something

as parents, we

moved around him

—getting more and more nervous

about the rubbish or the bins

meanwhile

our son, gradually maturing, became equipped

with an ability to observe and think independently

—almost every day

he asks stubborn questions

he says: Dad or Mom

but why adults

litter everywhere

right. These adults, so uncivilised

so unhygienic

so lacking in self-love and love of the environment

so shameless

and with so much disregard for their face

—we bore it for four years

until one day when I could no longer bear it

and was so upset that I said to my son:

you can now chuck rubbish anywhere from today onwards

like the adults

and my son, bewildered

said: Why?

I said there was no why because you were also an adult now

when my son, who had just finished his ice lolly, looking puzzled

chucked the little stick onto the ground

and accompanied it, just like that

with a spit of phlegm

I swallowed hard

and put my thumb up, to my son, now 6

I said: Well, son, you are right

that's the way you have to do this outside now

in the future

礼拜

上午，两家子人在大桥上偶遇
我们一家子要去公园放风筝
他们一家子要去基督堂做礼拜

两家子人都是那么彬彬有礼
互相点头，问候
然后温和地微笑，道别

我忍不住小声嘀咕
——这些年，他们家那印刷厂
不知道仿造了多少吨的假商标

我说，他们去做礼拜
是为了倾听牧师布道呢
还是去向上帝忏悔

我这没信仰的人的腰眼儿被妻子
用胳膊肘撞了一下
哈哈一笑，我瞥了瞥眼前那高高的十字架

Going to Church

in the morning, the two families met, by accident, on a bridge

we were going to fly the kite in a park

and they, going to a church

both families were so polite

nodding their heads and greeting

then saying goodbye, with a mild smile

I couldn't help mumbling

—the printer they had been running, for years

God knows how many tons of fake brands they had printed

I said: Are they going to church

to listen to the priest preach

or to make confessions to God?

my wife elbowed me, a non-believer

in my side

with a laugh, I glanced at the tall cross, right in front of me

剧场

台上灯光绚丽
台下，所有的人都在鼓掌
使劲喝彩，呐喊，尖叫

而我挤在黑暗中
感到毛骨悚然——
我太熟悉那些剧本了
惊恐的我，在四处
寻找出口

In the Theatre

the lights were brilliant on the stage
and, off stage, everyone was applauding
cheering as hard as they could, yelling, shrieking

and I, squeezed in the darkness
was horrified—
I was so familiar with the plays
a terrified me was looking for an exit
everywhere

天空

奇异的景象出现在大街上的天空
——日落时分，空中聚集了
一条由云朵儿铺就的宽阔彩带
难以数计的白云
自东向西，一小朵一小朵
像一片片闪光的鱼鳞
整齐而又绝对规则地铺向
霞光万丈的天边

"啊，多么漂亮的白云！"
"白云，我从来没有见过你
是这么的美丽！"
——背着小书包的儿子在造句
在向着天空稚拙地抒情
站在背后的我和妻子，被他的小手指引
也翘首发出了两声惊呼——
而我们随即羞愧地发现
整条大街上的所有人都没有抬头
只有接连几个被我们挡了道的人

不满地匆匆横了一眼这碍事的

神经兮兮的，一家子

The Sky

a strange spectacle appeared in the sky over the street

—sunset time, the sky was gathering

a broad ribbon of colours, strewn with clouds

countless white clouds

from the east to the west, small flowers of them

like shiny fish-scales

spreading, neatly and regularly

towards the edge of the sky, with tens of thousands of rays of glow

'oh, such beautiful white clouds!'

'white clouds that I have never seen

and you are so beautiful!'

—my little son, carrying a schoolbag, was making a sentence

being clumsily lyrical with the sky, in his childish way

and my wife, standing behind me and following his little pointing hand

also raised her head, with an exclamation or two—

then we were ashamed to find

that, of all the people on the street, no one raised his or her head

except a few, obstructed by us on their way

who glared at us with discontent and thought:

what a neurotic family!

纪念一种

府尹大人拍拍屁股走了
他在本州留下显赫的政绩
上省城游西湖，赴任去了

府尹大人学的是化工
曾经长期，工作于环保部门
他学以致用，再削尖脑袋
为本州争取到了一个
世界级的石化项目

府尹大人拍拍屁股走了
本州人民守着凭空飞来的
定时炸弹
再也睡不着觉——

他们在院子里扎稻草人
吐唾沫，掷飞镖
她们在手里绣布人
念咒语，戳心窝

——我能做什么呢

我只有用一个错词，造一个病句

——我说，本州人民永远纪念他

Commemoration of Sorts

the great prefect has left, patting his own hips

leaving his outstanding achievements in this prefecture

for the provincial capital, to tour the West Lake and to go to his new post

the great man's specialty is chemistry

for a long time, he has worked in environmental protection

he studied for practical use and he tried his hardest

to win a world-level project

for his own prefecture

the great prefect has left, patting his own hips

the people of the prefecture, though, are kept awake

by a time bomb

that has been flown in from nowhere——

they are plaiting a straw man in their backyards

they are spitting at him and throwing darts at him

and the women are embroidering a cloth man

cursing and jabbing at the heart of the cloth man

—but what can I do?

all I can do is use a wrong word and make a sick sentence   *

—I said: The people of this prefecture will always commemorate him

冷漠一种

早晨，在十字街口
瞥见一个人
——她在静候绿灯
而我不想挤出
形式主义的笑容
吐露，自己的言不由衷
——我低头，大踏步
闯红灯走了

傍晚，在家接听电话
一个暧昧的声音——
"我早认识你了，你也该
认识我一下呀……"

我听到自己的嘴里
随即滑出一句话，然后
撂下了话筒——
"不，这个冬天我再也
不想认识一个人了……"

A Kind of Coldness

in the morning, at the crossroads

I saw someone, in a glance

—she was quietly waiting for the lights to turn green

I didn't intend to reveal my own insincerity

by squeezing

a formalist smile

—I lowered my head and strode off

rushing the red lights

in the evening, I got a call

from a voice that sounded ambiguous—

'I have known you all along and you ought to

at least acknowledge it—'

I heard something slip

out of my own mouth before

I slammed the phone—

'no, I don't want to know anyone

anymore, not this winter…'

紫云英

父亲为我带来了紫云英
——这一竹篮子
纯天然的野菜
当我忍不住翻动它们
我触摸到了，滚动的露珠
星星点点的，新鲜泥巴

紫云英，童年的紫云英
在田野里到处举着
最朴素的小花——
如今它们依旧，低眉顺眼
可我直勾勾望着却发觉
那嫩绿，分明透着一股子的骄傲

我向儿子描述起田野里的紫云英
——我曾在紫云英丛中割鹅草
——我曾在紫云英上大翻跟头
——我还是吃着紫云英长大的
而幼稚的他猛扑过去，嘴里叼起了一束
那咀嚼的模样，多么像田埂上的小牛犊

Milk Vetch

when Father brought me the milk vetch
—a bamboo basket
of purely natural wild greens
I couldn't help turning them over
I touched the rolling dewdrops
little stars, with fresh mud

milk vetch, milk vetch of my childhood
raised everywhere in the field
their simplest flowers—
they remain submissive, with downcast eyes
but, in my direct gaze, I discovered
that their tender greenness revealed pride of a kind

I described the milk vetch in the field to my son
—I used to cut the goose grass in the clusters of milk vetch
—I used to turn somersaults over the milk vetch
—and I grew up eating the milk vetch
and the little one rushed over, putting a bunch between his lips
the way he chewed it resembled so much a calf on a ridge between the
     fields

为祖母照相

难得与祖母见一回面
这一回，她突然提出让我
为她照张相片

我拿出相机——
已经八十八岁的祖母
像个小女孩
她羞涩地梳头，换衣服
然后又去照镜子

我举着相机——
祖母说，可要照得好看些
她像个小女孩一样
对着我开心地笑

我摁下快门——
祖母说，多照几张吧
帮我选张最好看的
还要能放大一点

我猛地愣怔住——
祖母笑得灿烂，说
都活了这么久，不定
哪天突然就要走了
我得先照张相，好好备着

Taking a Photograph of My Grandma

it's hard to see my grandma these days
this time round, though, she, unexpectedly, asked me
to take a photograph of her

I produced the camera—
grandma, now over 80
like a little girl
shyly, she combed her hair and changed her clothes
before she took a look in the mirror

I raised the camera—
grandma said: Take a good one
like a little girl
she smiled happily for me

I pressed the shutter—
grandma said: Take a few more
and select the best
something that could be enlarged

I was taken aback—
grandma's smile was brilliant, she said
I have lived this long and I may

have to go one day

I need to get ready, with a photograph

女邻居

楼上新来了一位女邻居
浓眉，乌溜乌溜的大眼睛
皮肤黝黑，但却光彩照人
陌生的女邻居
上楼下楼，总是冲我笑
笑得我胸中怦怦然

终于有一回，女邻居
不仅笑盈盈露出了
一副漂亮的白牙
"你真的不认识我了吗？"
她正下楼，居高临下
质问一脸茫然无辜的我

我愣怔住，傻笑着摇头
瞥见她身后跑下来俩小孩
"我是他们的妈妈呀！
呵呵，我减肥了——
两个月，减掉二十二公斤肥肉了呀！"
她向我透露这一惊天大秘密

噢——我的老天
我张大了嘴巴，久久难以合拢
——这楼上的肥婆
多年来，我从没拿正眼
打量过的丑陋肥婆
居然有此鬼斧神工的大行动

"太恐怖了！一下子减去
这么多，你的心脏受得了吗？"
我盯着她，重新仔细打量
"没有事的啦，从前在老家
我就是这么瘦的呀——
我管它什么心脏，漂亮最要紧的啦！"

女邻居，忽然漂亮得像是
印度美少女的女邻居
带着俩混血儿似的小屁孩
她朝我挥挥手，开心地下楼而去
——留下惊愕的我，目睹走廊那头
那扭动的小屁股，那两支飘荡的大裤管

My Next Door Neighbour

upstairs, there came a new neighbour

with bushy eyebrows and very black eyes

although she had dark skin, she looked gorgeous

my stranger as a neighbour

whether going upstairs or downstairs, would smile to me

and cause my heart to miss a beat

until one day when she

revealed, in a glittering smile

a full set of beautiful teeth

'you really can't recognise me now?'

coming downstairs, in her commanding position

she demanded, and I looked completely innocent

I stood in a daze, shaking my head, with a stupid smile

and saw, in a glance, two kids running down behind her

'well, I'm their mother!

ha, ha, ha, I am on a diet—

and, in two months, I've lost 22 kilos of fat!'

she revealed the sky-big secret

ah, well—heavens

my mouth agape, hard to close for a long time

—the fat woman upstairs

over the years I've never properly looked

at this ugly fat aunty

who has taken a big action of such superlative craftsmanship

'so terrifying! Can your heart stand all that

with so much lost in one go?'

staring at her, I, carefully, sized her up again

'well, nothing serious. At my old home I used to be

this thin—

who gives a damn about the heart as long as one stays pretty?'

my neighbour, suddenly as beautiful

as a beautiful Indian girl

took her two kids, like those of mixed-blood

and, with a wave of her hand towards me, happily went downstairs

—leaving me, flabbergasted, watching the little swaying hips

at the other end of the corridor, inside those big dancing trouser-legs

修辞

母亲一生胆小，并且固执
CT 检查显示她右肺的中叶已经
萎缩，快整个儿坏掉了
可她坚决不做摘除手术
让所有在场的医生，都无计可施
——她把头摇得像拨浪鼓
说，我宁愿咳嗽，天天咳嗽
宁愿一直咳到再也咳不出来

怎么办呢，只有暂且回家
我陪母亲走出医院——
路过小公园，我随手
撩拨了一下那棵小树
抓住斜逸出来的一个枝条
说，姆妈你看这几片树叶
就好比是这片枯叶
它要掉了，得提前给摘下来
有五片树叶呀，就摘一片
你看，一下子就好了

我轻轻摘下那片枯叶

在母亲面前摊开手掌

一片枯叶，小小的一个比方

谁知，母亲停下了脚步

她捡起那片枯叶，她在

冬日早晨八九点钟的阳光下

仔细端详，而眼神里

似乎没有了那份坚决

试探着再前进一步，我说

——姆妈，从两根肋骨中间探进去

就好比是窗户的两根铁栅栏

医生伸进去两个手指头

摘下这片树叶，以后

再也不用担心它掉下来

而你每天的咳嗽……

我的话还没说完，母亲打断了我

她咬了咬腮帮子，说

——那好吧，就把它给摘掉算了

Rhetoric

mother has been timid, all her life, and stubborn

her CT scan has shown that the middle lobe of her right lung

shrunken to the degree of dysfunction

but she firmly refused to have it removed in an operation

making all the doctors present clueless

according to her, she'd rather cough, on a daily basis

till she could not cough any more

what can we do but just go home, for the moment

I, accompanying my mother, walked out of the hospital—

as we went past the small park, I, with a casual wave of my hand

teasing the small tree

grabbed hold of a branch that came sticking out

and said: Mom, look at these leaves

it's like this withered one

when it's about to fall, you have to remove it in advance

if there are five, you have to take one

and then you see, everything is fine

gently, I took down the leaf

and held out my palm, in front of Mom

a leaf, a tiny little metaphor

little did I expect that she'd stop in her tracks

she picked up the leaf and she

in the morning sunshine at around 8 or 9

took a careful look, the kind of resolution

seeming to have gone out of her eyes

venturing further, I said

—Mom, poking between the two ribs

like the two iron bars in a window

the doctor would put in his two fingers

to take down the leaf and, afterwards

you won't have to worry that it might fall

and your daily coughing...

before I could finish, Mom interrupted me

and, clenching her teeth, said

—all right then, I'll have it removed and leave it at that

一个笑话

晚餐的中途，杨渡说要给我
讲一个笑话——

今天中午，我的同学张高崎
把圆珠笔插在课桌上
接着他去拔，可怎么也拔不出来了

——我停止咀嚼，张嘴看着
对面正读小学六年级的儿子
一直等待，他的下文

然而下文却没有了
——儿子说爸爸，你不觉得好笑吗

这有什么好笑的——
我这么说了半句，突然一愣怔
我不能确定，或者说不敢相信
一个小孩子能够
从这么个日常的细节中
看出笑话来

你不觉得这是一个笑话吗——
儿子笑嘻嘻地看着我的眼睛
他说，我的同学张高崎
——他的东西被卡住了
都拔不出来啦，不好笑吗

我咳嗽了一下，用漫不经心的眼神
看了看我的儿子
看了看他那张古怪的笑脸
我当然没有笑，还板起了脸——
我说，这么个小事儿有什么好笑的
好啦好啦，别废话
食不言寝不语，赶紧吃饭

风卷残云般完事，进书房
关门，想起刚才惊险的一幕
我再也，把持不住了
——那还真是
一个，笑话

A Joke

halfway through dinner, Yang Du said that he'd like to tell me
a joke—

at noon today, my classmate Zhang Gaoqi
inserted his ballpoint pen in his school desk
then, when he tried to pull it out he couldn't however hard he tried

—I stopped chewing, watching him with an open mouth
this son of mine studying at Grade 6 in a primary school
waiting to hear what happened next
but there was nothing that happened next
—my son said: Dad, didn't you find it funny?

what's there so funny about—
I had not finished what I had wanted to say before I was surprised
as I was not sure or I did not have the courage to believe
that a teenage boy could
possibly see a joke
in such an ordinary detail

didn't you find that funny—
grinning, my son looked into my eyes
he said, my classmate Zhang Gaoqi

—his thing got stuck

and he couldn't pull it out. Wasn't that funny enough?

I coughed and, casually, I took a glance

at my son

at that strange face of his

of course, I didn't laugh; instead, my face hardened—

I said, there wasn't anything funny about that, such a small thing

well, well, no more nonsense

eat your meal and quick, no talking while eating or sleeping, as the

    wisdom goes

after making a clean sweep of my food and entering my study

with the door closed behind me, I, on recalling the episode

could barely contain my mirth

—it was a joke

a real one

小鼹鼠

午餐时，她坐我对面
小小的一个细节让我不由得
屏住了呼吸——

她放下筷子，摆整齐
放下饭碗，摆端正
伸出左手
去抽一张餐巾纸
之后用双手举着它
凑近自己的左脸
原来，脸颊上粘了小半粒米饭
像捕捉一只笨拙的蚊子
她成功了，之后用纸包裹了
那饭粒，折叠妥帖
再用纸团去，郑重其事地擦脸
擦刚才粘过饭粒的位置
来回反复擦了四下
最后在桌面，摆好纸团
一切停当，才分别
端起碗筷，继续用餐

——猛地觉得，她多么像一只小鼹鼠

虽然我没见过鼹鼠

甚至，根本不知道

那鼹鼠到底长什么样

我只知道，打小她就

喜欢鼹鼠，痴迷于所有

有关鼹鼠的图片与文字

而此时此刻，倘若

我打一个突兀的比喻

说她像一只小鼹鼠

我想她一定不会，反对

十二岁的小丫头，她喊我舅舅

某一天，循着我的启发

她突然成了诗人，哗的一声

一下子爆发出那么多诗

很多很多虚无缥缈的诗

很多很多惊心动魄的诗

似乎是为了让很多很多诗人气绝

——我盯着眼前这只小鼹鼠

虚弱的小鼹鼠

挑食的小鼹鼠

机警的小鼹鼠

两只眼睛大大的小鼹鼠
天真又无比犀利的小鼹鼠
忍不住，打了个激灵——

多么漂亮的小鼹鼠
多少年之后
在某一个日子
她将会漂洋过海
带我去往，一个很远很远的美丽国度

A Mole

at lunchtime, she sat opposite me
when a small detail made me catch
my breath—

she put down her chopsticks, side by side in a neat row
she put down her bowl and set it right
holding out her left hand
to pull out a tissue
before she raised it, with both her hands
and approached her left cheek
the way she went for a clumsy mosquito
where half a grain of rice got stuck
she succeeded and, subsequently, wrapped it up
with the tissue, folding it properly
as she used the tissue to wipe her cheek most seriously
where the rice had got stuck
and repeatedly for four times
before she finally put down the roll of tissue on the table
it was not till then that, things done, she began
picking up her bowl and went on with her meal

—suddenly, I found her so much like a mole
although I have never seen one

I do not even know

what a mole looks like

all I know is that she, from when she was a little girl

has liked moles all along, obsessed with all

pictures and words

and, here and now, if

I made an abrupt analogy

saying that she was like a mole

she would not, I don't think, dislike it

this girl, twelve years of age, calls me Uncle, a maternal one

one day, following my lead

she became a sudden poet, with a bang

bursting out in so many poems

many an imaginary one

many a breath-taking one

as if deliberately to upset many a poet

—I gazed at this mole

this weak little mole

this picky mole

this vigilant mole

this little mole with two big eyes

innocent little mole with unmatched sharpness

I couldn't help feeling a sudden shiver—

such a beautiful mole

in years to come

on a certain day

she will drift across the seas

taking me, to a far, far country of beauty

我醒着

我醒着——
黑夜里，床在漂浮
漂浮出了窗外
窗外雾霾笼罩

无声息的冷雨
冷雨下在广场
广场上醒着裸露的球形路灯
球形路灯在广场上漂浮

我醒着——
我睁开的双眼，就是两只湿漉漉的路灯
冷雨一直在无声息地下
雾霾绝望地笼罩黑暗的广场

我是一个诚实的人
此刻，我只想说
我醒着——
至于其他，请允许我不说出

I Stayed Awake

I stayed awake—
in the dark night, my bed was set afloat
out the window
outside, everything was shrouded in a haze

a cold rain, soundless
a cold rain that was raining on the square
on the square, the naked ball-shaped streetlights were awake
the ball-shaped streetlights were afloat on the square

I stayed awake—
my opened eyes were two wet streetlights
the cold rain had been raining, without a sound
the haze shrouding the dark square with despair

I am an honest man
right now, all I want to say is
I stayed awake—
as for the rest, please allow me not to voice

水墨中国

这是怎样的一个国家呀
你一声叹息
颓然靠向墙壁，眉头紧锁

我微笑，说
水墨中国呀

你一愣怔——
曾经，你在水墨画上浸淫多年

水，形容词
墨，形容词
具体说，都是状态词与贬义词
——我解释

水墨中国，无关水墨画
你鬼哭狼嚎般大笑
举起中指吼说，水墨中国，我操哇

Water and Ink China

what sort of a country is that?
you sighed
in dejection, leaning against the wall, knitting your brows

I, smiling, said
ah, well, it's water and ink China

you were taken aback—
for years, you were steeped in water and ink paintings

water, an adjective
ink, an adjective, too
to be concrete, they both were modal and derogatory terms
—I explained

Chinese water and ink had nothing to do with water and ink paintings
you laughed, out loud, like a devil crying
raising the middle finger, you screamed: Oh, fuck water and ink China!

咽喉炎

许多年前，我曾一度为咽喉炎
所折磨——我的意思是说此刻
咽喉炎早已经离我远去，只是
它给我留下了刻骨铭心的记忆

如今我们的朋友不幸患上咽喉炎
她描述求生不得求死不能的症状
——对我们说她经常难受得都想
掐住自己的喉咙，一把掐死自己

可我们实在忍不住要捧腹大笑——
因为我们的朋友，她明明白白指出
自己得的不是咽喉炎，而是阴道炎
"该死的阴道炎！"她还大声诅咒

我们的朋友，她可绝对不是个幽默的人
而这次说得咬牙切齿，无论如何都不会
故意幽默如此——那么唯一的可能就是
口误，该死的口误，是非常要命的口误

在街角，我们看着她愤愤甩手走远
忙不迭笑得弯腰，蹲下去泪花四溅
并且我们都忍不住非要想多了——
所有的口误，应该都不是无缘无故

Pharyngitis

many years ago I suffered from
pharyngitis—I mean that it was a long
time ago although it has left me a bone
carving memory

our friend, unfortunately, is now suffering from it, too
she describes the condition as something that makes her want to die
—and she told us that it is so insufferable that, sometimes, grabbing herself
by the throat, she wishes to strangle herself to death

but we couldn't help splitting our sides with laughter—
because our friend told us in no uncertain terms
that she suffered from vaginitis, not pharyngitis
'damn it!', she cursed, in a loud voice

our friend is not a funny person
gnawing her teeth when she said it; it can't have been a deliberate
attempt at humour—the only possibility then must be
a slip of tongue. Damn it, a fatal one at that

in the corner of a street, we saw her walk away, angrily
as we, bent double with laughter, squatting with laughing tears

were unable to contain ourselves from a further thought—

that all such slips of tongue might not have been for no reason at all

他们谈论米沃什时都说些什么

那年的那一天早晨
我端着早餐来到了几位诗人中间
他们围着桌子，一边早餐
一边窃窃私语

我渐渐听懂了，在努力拼贴出
一些零碎的语词之后
——他们把米沃什的诗篇当作了
《圣经》，每一位脸上都泛着
异样的神采与光芒

我进而还原的历史——
在昨夜，他们彻夜未眠
像干革命，或其他的地下工作
他们谈论米沃什直至东方既白

他们在谈论米沃什时都说些什么
此事原本我打算不再关心
然而不巧，我还是听到了关键之处

——他们反复说到了米沃什的语言
甚至是，米沃什的语感

多年以来，那个早晨
一直让我耿耿于怀——
因为我来到了某个秘密团伙中间
太过冒昧——对于我的过错
我几乎要笑弯了腰
——前不久的那晚，面对一位翻译家
我笑得最放肆，最终笑出了两颗眼泪
我告诉翻译家，那个团伙的诗人们
既不懂波兰语，也懂不了几个英文单词

What Did They Say When They Were Talking About Miłosz

that morning that year

I, with my breakfast, went to the poets

surrounding the table, having their breakfast

as they were chatting among themselves, in a subdued voice

it gradually dawned on me after I made an attempt at piecing together

a few fragmentary words

—they were treating poems by Miłosz

as the Bible, each and every one of their faces lit

with a peculiar light and look

I further worked out the history—

last night they must have been sleepless all night

as if engaging in a revolution or some sort of underground work

talking about Miłosz till the day broke

I didn't intend to show interest

in what they said when talking about Miłosz

but it so happened that I did catch the crucial point

—they kept mentioning Miłosz's language

even his sense of language

for many years, I have very much taken that morning
to heart—
because I had arrived at a secret brotherhood of some sort
so presumptuously—I was bent double with laughter
at my mistake

—one evening not so long ago, I, in the translator's presence
laughed most uncontrollably till I shed two tears
I told him that the poets of the brotherhood
knew no Polish and, at best, just a few English words

三叔的遗言

三叔过世了，有关我
他只留下了一句遗言

他仔细交代三婶说："记得以后
种了菜，要经常寄到城里去……"

三叔过世了，经常
伸筷子夹菜的时候我的眼泪会夺眶而出

Third Uncle's Last Words

before Third Uncle died, these were the last words
he said about me

carefully, he said to Third Aunty, 'Don't forget
to mail vegetables to the city when you grow them...'

after his death, I often burst into tears
when I reach for the vegetables with my chopsticks

坏习惯

曾经有多少次，在街头
在各类公共场合
我为发现自己裤子的前门没有拉上而羞愧

不错，我人到中年
记忆力在大踏步后退
可我一直视裤子的前门为要地
却又为何频频失守

终于有一天我找到了问题之症结
——它无关记忆
而仅仅是因为坏习惯

——我的家居生活已经太久
我的家居生活太过随便
养成了从来不关前门的坏习惯

Bad Habit

on many occasions, in the streets
or in various public places
I am ashamed to find my pants, my front door, unzipped

right. For a middle-aged man like me
my memory is striding backwards
but why does my front door, a strategic point
fail so often to close?

one day, finally, I found the key to the problem
—it had nothing to do with memory
it's just a bad habit

—I have been so used to staying indoors
and so casual with myself at home
I have formed a bad habit of never closing my front door

愤怒

轿车缓缓行进——
我们一路高雅的话题
被马路两边的园林工人们所打断

他们穿着一律的工作服
举着一律铮亮的园林剪
把那些蓬蓬勃勃的树苗
修剪得如此整齐又划一

我的愤怒油然而生
手指着那些暴徒——
嘴里猛然喷发出最原生态的秽语

而你顿时减速
——在后视镜里
你仔细地，瞥我一眼
满脸的诧异

Anger

our car was going slowly—
our elegant conversation on the way
was cut short by the gardeners on either side of the street

they were wearing uniform uniforms
and, with their uniform shining garden shears
were trimming the robust saplings
in such a neat order

that I flared up
and, pointing at the thugs—
I unleashed a string of the most pristine expletives

and you suddenly reduced the speed
—looking so puzzled
as you took a careful glance at me
in the rear-view mirror

危如累卵

阅读分析课上
碰到这生僻的成语
我觉得有必要做一番解释——

举起双手比画出一大堆东西
我说假若把一块块鹅卵石
这样地叠起来，叠得高高的
然后大家来想象一下
它们将会有，怎样的结局

——几乎所有孩子都眼睁睁看着
我比画出的这么一大堆东西
可是他们流露出的表情
没有达到我所预期的效果

此时此刻，一脸疑惑的我
目睹了一脸疑惑的一位女生
她怯怯地说出了自己的疑惑——
"老师，卵不是鹅卵石啊！
这里的卵，应该是蛋吧？"

这位小心翼翼的女生
她没说到一半，我就不由得暗自惊呼
惊讶于自己的如此昏聩了

"对对对！这里的卵指的就是蛋
——真是见鬼，我怎么扯鹅卵石去了？"
我大笑，告诉这些可爱的孩子们
老师之所以出现如此低级的口误
是因为他们经常在作文里写到鹅卵石
而又老是把卵字写错或把它的声母搞错
但同时，也因为我的年纪和满头的白发

我用两个手指头，对着自己的脑袋
敲了又敲，我告诉他们
到我这个年纪，这玩意儿里面
早已经是——
危如累卵

Luan

in a class about reading and analysis
when this strange idiom, 'as dangerous as stacked eggs', came up
I found it necessary to explain—

holding up my hands in a gesture indicative of a heap of things
I said that if one stacked up goose-egg pebbles
like that, to a great height
what sort of end it would come to
can anyone imagine?

—nearly all the kids were staring
at the heap I gestured about
but the way they looked
was not what I had expected

at that moment, I, with a puzzled look
witnessed how a girl student, also with a puzzled look
timidly offered her own bewilderment—
'but, Teacher, *luan* is not pebbles!
here, aren't they eggs?'

even before the careful girl finished

half of what she had to say, I had suppressed a cry of surprise

as I was shocked by my own stupidity

'right, right, right! The *luan* here refers to eggs

—bloody hell! How could I have possibly talked about pebbles?

I burst out laughing as I said to those lovely kids

that the reason their teacher had made such a low-level slip of tongue

was that they'd often written about pebbles in their homework

and had always got the word 'luan' or its initial consonant wrong

but, at the same time, it was also because of my age and my headful of

      white hair

I knocked at my head, with two fingers

and knocked at it again, telling them

that, at my age, it was

long—

full of *luan*

大清早杀个人

大清早，站在十字路口
等候绿灯亮起
眼前，一辆黑色轿车的驾驶室里
骨碌碌丢出一只农夫山泉的空瓶子
刹那间，我想起某一天下午
也是站在购物中心前的这个十字路口
也是站在这个位置
也是眼前那个位置
约莫六七米开外
一辆乳白色轿车，驾驶室的玻璃徐徐降下
一只白皙漂亮年轻的手，伸出来
滴溜溜丢下一只加多宝的铁罐子
在清洁的街道中央咣当咣当跳舞
刹那间，我真想操起一把雪亮的西瓜刀
追上去，在那个美女还没来得及缩回那只手之前
手起刀落，把它齐刷刷给剁下

那辆黑色轿车，黑旋风一般冲过去了
紧接着另一辆蓝色轿车在它屁股后头
自西向东冲过，紧接着

又一辆红色轿车冲过

——它的左前轮恰好轧上了空瓶子

巨大的力量，让空瓶子一下子干瘪

让它的红色瓶盖朝我发射

精确击中我裸露的小腿

我的杀气霍然升腾

想象中，雪亮的西瓜刀再度操起

我奋起直追——

我要追上在街道中央丢下空瓶子的那个司机

这回我不是剁手

我要砍了他的狗头

但是，我又怎么追得上那个畜生呢

大清早，站在十字路口

绿灯终于亮起

我满脸杀气，杀气腾腾走过斑马线

一边在心里恶毒地诅咒

——追杀他不及，不如

干脆让他在前方，撞×

I Wanted to Kill Someone Early One Morning

early one morning, when I stood at the crossroads

waiting for the lights to turn green

an empty bottle of Nongfu Spring came rolling out

of a black car, from the driver's seat, right before my nose

in an instant, I was reminded of an afternoon

when I also stood at the same crossroads in front of a shopping centre

also in this spot

the same spot right under my nose

about six or seven metres away

a creamy car had its window slowly winded down

as a pretty white hand extended itself out

and let drop, clicking and clanging, an iron can of Jia Duo Bao

that started dancing, bam bam, in the middle of a clean street

in that instant, I wished I had a shining watermelon knife

and gave that car a chase, cutting off the hand

before the pretty woman withdrew it, with just one hack

the black car rushed off, like a black whirlwind

closely followed by a blue car, bumper to bumper

from the west to the east, and closely

followed by another red car

—its left front wheel crushing right onto the empty bottle

so that, with a tremendous force, the bottle was flattened

and its red cap shot at me

so accurately that it hit me on my naked shin

I became instantly murderous

in my imagination, I raised the same watermelon knife

and gave a chase—

I'd chase till I caught the driver who had thrown the bottle

and, on this occasion, I didn't want to cut off his hand

I wanted to cut off his dog head

however, how could I possibly get to the brute?

early in the morning, while standing at the crossroads

and the lights finally turned green

I, with a murderous face, murderously crossed the zebra crossing

cursing, with venom, at heart, wishing

that he would crash into something somewhere down there if

I didn't end up killing him

晃荡

他穿一件小背心，光膀子
走在半上午的阳光里
腋下夹一床卷筒状的小棉被
双手小心翼翼把它箍住，生怕滑落

公园边，我与他迎面相遇
大冬天的，可看神情
他一点儿都不冷
只是特别珍惜那床脏兮兮的小棉被

我俩错身而过时，我瞅见了
他那两条健壮的古铜色大腿
以及其上茂密的黑丛林
以及黑丛林中，一对不住晃荡着的硕大睾丸

Dangling

wearing a singlet, and bare-armed
he was walking in the late morning sun
with a roll of cotton-padded quilt under his arm
holding it with both hands, fearful it might fall

at the edge of a park, I ran into him head-on
it was the middle of the winter but he didn't look
as if he were cold
except that he took special care of his dirty quilt

just when we went past each other, I saw
his solid thighs, bronze-coloured
and the cluster of black bush over them
and, in the bush, his huge balls that kept dangling

草坪

在松江的上海对外经贸大学
欧阳昱带头一脚踩上草坪
客随主便，我也犹犹豫豫
踩了上去

草坪用来干吗的
欧阳说，草坪就是用来走的嘛
在澳洲，大家一看到草坪
就踩上去，就走过去
或者坐下来，躺下来
你看，多舒服

是的，多舒服
小时候我在乡村长大
赤脚，到处走，到处跑
尤其雨天或雨后
脚趾与草茎，脚底与草茎
亲密接触，令人痒痒

此刻，欧阳的皮凉鞋

鞋底儿完全被雨后的草坪吞没
他的脚后跟，沾染了新鲜泥巴

为何不干脆脱下两只皮凉鞋
拎着走
我大胆的想象被打断
哈哈哈
欧阳爆发出大笑
招牌式的三笑，洪亮又短促
哈哈哈
欧阳用手指着不远处，这边和那边
你看，在国内，所有人都绕着草坪走
你看，你看
哈哈哈

与欧阳一道穿走过几个大草坪
末了，我们各自把两只脚连同皮凉鞋
伸进草坪中的两个坑里，仔细濯洗

草坪之水清兮，可以濯我缨
草坪之水浊兮，可以濯我足
拔出双脚，我抬头四顾
不由得莞尔，不由得蓦然一惊

在上海对外经贸大学师生眼里
欧阳教授恐怕是一头经常穿走在
草坪之上的恐龙
澳洲文明，在松江
无比野蛮

The Lawn

at SUIBE in Songjiang
Ouyang Yu took the lead by stepping onto a lawn
as his guest, I followed him, but hesitantly
I trod it, too

what is the lawn used for?
Ouyang said. It's meant for walking on
in Australia, whenever people see a lawn
they step onto it, crossing it
sitting down or lying down on it
you see, so comfortable

that's right, so comfortable
when I grew up in a village
I, barefoot, walked, and ran everywhere
particularly in a rain or after the rain
my toes and my soles in intimate touch
with stems of grass, getting itchy

right now, the soles of Ouyang's leather sandals
were swallowed up by the lawn after a rain
his heels freshly muddy

why, then, doesn't he take off his shoes

and hold them in his hands?

but my imagination was interrupted

ha, ha, ha

Ouyang burst out laughing

in his patent manner, sonorous and short

ha, ha, ha

as he pointed at a spot not far off, here and there, and said:

look, in China, everyone skirts around the lawn

look, look

ha, ha, ha

walking with Ouyang across a number of vast lawns

till, in the end, we put our feet, along with the leather sandals

in two waterholes in the lawn, carefully washing them

ah, the clean water of the lawn, washing my tassels

ah, the muddy water of the lawn, washing my feet

as I pulled out my feet, I looked around

I was taken aback, with a smile

in the eyes of staff and students at SUIBE

Translator's note—SUIBE, short for Shanghai University of International Business and Economics.

professor Ouyang may have been a monster

constantly walking across the lawns

Australian civilisation in Songjiang

is matchlessly savage

诗与屎

诗被辱骂为屎
是诗受到的最大侮辱
最多侮辱
作为诗人
我无话可说
那些人不也穿戴着屎吗
平常我粪土黄金
黄金也是无辜的

而作为诗人
我得承认
诗与屎
关键时刻确实一致
比如我无论多么忙碌
却忙不过屎，以屎为大
却忙不过诗，以诗为大
屎与诗同样势不可挡

比如刚才，我在修订一份重要且急用的讲稿
可又不得不丢下讲稿急匆匆跑去坐到马桶上

真是无比畅快呀

一泡金黄的屎和一首金黄的诗

同时诞生

Poetry and Shit

that poetry is abused as shit is
the worst of all the abuses
poetry suffers
and as a poet
I am speechless
don't those people wear shit?
as a rule, I shit gold
but gold is innocent

but as a poet
I must admit
poetry (shi) and shit (shi)
are really identical, in critical moments
for example, I am never as busy
as my shit, and I treat it with utmost importance
I'm never as busy as my poetry, which I also treat with utmost importance
both shit and poetry equally unstoppable

for another example, while I was revising an important, urgently needed
     speech
I had to put it down to get to the toilet in a hurry
the downloading so pleasurable

as a golden poo and a golden poem

were simultaneously created

闯入

最初闯入的肯定是夜雨
并非润物细无声
它噼噼啪啪
滴滴答答
可我的雷达没有启动
关键是一对男女
在楼下街道，他俩真切
恰好又不太清晰
的对话
每一句
都砸在
我耳畔
那女，嚣张得很
那男，是个怂货
对着对着，怂货竟然哭了
边哭边小声央求
他们撑着伞还是淋着雨
他妈的他们还有完没完
四点零四分
骤地响起一声喇叭

哦，他妈的原来在车里呀

可那怂货，是否在车门外湿着

我坐起身想去窗边查看

却与自己较了劲

偏又躺下

不理那对男女

我盼望他们尽快

在雷达区消失

然而他妈的没有

嚣张继续嚣张

怂货继续怂货

唉，难道非要我提一根铁棍下楼吗

四点三十九分

低分贝且低频率的古怪声响

席地而来

进入雷达区

天哪，该死的压缩垃圾车

它不是延迟时间了吗

那一次我闯上门去投诉之后

它不是都延迟至五点三十分进来的吗

由于垃圾车闯入

砰的一声

那对男女关门大吉

吱地开车走了
我的天，垃圾车缓缓推进
呜呜呜呜，呜呜呜呜
它将蛮横滞留雷达区一小时
我的周末好梦计划
彻底黄了

Storming In

the first thing that stormed in must have been the night rain

not the kind that moistened things soundlessly

as it went pitapat

and drip, drip, drip

but my radar was not switched on

the key, though, was a man and a woman

were in the street below, their authentic

dialogue

wasn't very clear

although each and every sentence

struck

my ears

the woman was quite aggressive

and the man, a wimp

as they went on, the wimp burst into tears

begging in a low voice as he cried

one wasn't sure if they were holding an umbrella or were being rained

fuck! Is there going to be an end to all that?

at 4.04am

a horn suddenly went off

oh, I see, the fuckwits were in a car

but one isn't sure if the wimp was being rained outside it

I sat up, wanting to see what's going on out the window

but I lay back

wrestling with myself

trying to ignore them

and hoping they'd soon finish

and disappear from my radar

but they weren't even fucking finishing

the aggressive one went on being aggressive

and the wimp, being a wimp

oh, my, should I go downstairs with an iron rod or what?

at 4.39am

the weird noise, in low decibels and low frequency

came sweeping

onto my radar

heavens! It's the damned compression garbage truck

weren't they put off to a later time?

after I stormed in their door last time and complained

weren't they put off till 5.30am?

because of the intrusion of the garbage truck

the man and the woman slammed

their door

and started off with a screechy sound

my God, the garbage truck was slowly

booming along

as it would have to stay, arrogantly, in my radar area

thoroughly destroying

my plan for a weekend of good dreams

外地司机

打车的时候
我喜欢跟外地司机聊几句
本地司机都板着个臭脸
外地司机则把亲切二字写在脸上

这不，又遇上个亲切的
我说师傅老家哪儿
他说许昌
我说哎哟，许昌啊，好地方
他说，哪里哪里
我说许都嘛，挟天子以令诸侯
他说，您还知道这个
我说不仅知道，十多年前还亲自去过

拐弯时师傅突然话锋一转
他说家里有二十多亩田地，全种了小麦
真是踏破铁鞋无觅处
我正愁买不到正宗的农家麦粉呢
我这人上辈子都没怎么吃麦粉
一听那么多小麦，脑子里一片金黄，眼睛亮了

我激动地说，许昌那儿环境没污染是吧

师傅沉默片刻

他说，我们那村跟另一个村中间有一条河

我说哦，那敢情好，正好用来灌溉

师傅再次沉默片刻

然后咬牙，说哪里呀，上游有个天杀的造纸厂

我一声惊呼

师傅叹气说，我们两个村庄的人

许多许多都是脑子里统一长瘤哇

深夜会客归来

外地司机让我

打了一个哆嗦

Cabdrivers That Weren't Locals

when I went out in a cab

I preferred to chat with cabdrivers that weren't locals

cabdrivers that were locals had wooden faces that stank

while the non-local cabdrivers had kindness written all over their faces

exactly what happened just now, another kind one

I said: Master, where is your old home based?

he said: Xuchang

I said: Wow, that's a good place

he said: Not really

I said: It used to be the capital where the Emperor was overpowered to
      command the nobles

he said: How did you know about that?

I said: Not only that but I have been there a decade or so before

while doing a turn, Master changed his subject

saying that he had twenty-odd *mu* of land at home, all grown with wheat

to me, that is perfect as I am looking everywhere

for authentic peasant-grown wheat flour

I didn't have much of that in my previous life

my mind turned golden and my eyes lit up as soon as I heard of so much
      wheat

excitedly, I said: There is no pollution around Xuchang, right?

Master went silent, for a minute

before he said: There's a river between our village and another village

I said: That's good; it can be used for irrigation purposes

Master went briefly silent again

trying to bite his teeth, he said: No, but there is a horrible paper mill

    upstream

I cried in surprise

Master sighed and said: Of the people in these two villages

many have grown brain tumors

coming home late at night, after meeting my friends

the cabdriver that was not a local

was giving me the creeps

见微知著

最近我每天的早课是吃三颗
来自云南大山深处的薄皮核桃

刚才，我吃到第二颗
妻子来了客厅
向我伸手
我取出壳里仅剩的四分之一颗核桃仁
放入她手心

拿钳子剥第三颗时
妻子去了厨房
我享用完毕
咂嘴一想
破例又掏出了第四颗

几分钟后我去餐厅早餐
妻子涨红了脸
我说，干吗呢
她那副眼神看起来挺遥远
她说，你是个自私的人

我怎么就是个自私的人了呢
好不容易问出答案
原来不关第四颗核桃的事儿
妻子说，我吃东西的时候
不是经常都送一份到你书桌吗
我说，是啊，怎么啦
妻子说，那你怎么只给自己剥核桃

我无言以对
我想说，我没时间
我想说，你可以去剥十颗
可我没有
我只是承认，说是啊，我是个自私的人
且又重复一句，说对呀，我就是个自私的人

吃完早餐我照例摞筷去书房
出餐厅的一刹那
想起我已经好多年没洗过碗了
略一沉思，继续迈步
我对自己说，对呀，我就是个自私的人

The Little Things

for morning prayers, I now eat three
thin-skinned walnuts that come from the depths of mountains in Yunnan

just now, when I got to the second
my wife came to the sitting-room
her hand held out to me
I took out the remaining one fourth of the kernel
and put it in the heart of her hand

when, with a pair of pliers, I cracked the third
my wife went into the kitchen
finishing it
I had a think, smacking my lips
and, breaking my own rules, took out another one

a few minutes after, when I went into the kitchen for breakfast
my wife's face was flushed red
I said: What's the matter?
she looked remote
and she said: You are selfish

how can I be selfish?
I managed, though, to extract an answer

for it had nothing to do with the fourth walnut

she said: When I eat something

I always take it to your desk

I said: That's right. What's wrong then?

she said: But why did you crack the walnuts only for yourself?

I was speechless

I had wanted to say: I had no time

I had wanted to say: But you could crack ten

but I didn't

I just had to admit, saying: Yes, I'm selfish

and I repeated, saying: Right, I really am selfish

after breakfast, I went to my study, putting down the chopsticks as usual

but in the instant in which I went out of the kitchen

the thought came to me that I had not done the dishes for years

after dwelling on it for a bit, I continued to step out

and said to myself: Right, I really am selfish